HURRICANE DESTRUCTION
in
SOUTH CAROLINA

HURRICANE DESTRUCTION
in
SOUTH CAROLINA

Hell and High Water

TOM RUBILLO

THE
History
PRESS

Published by The History Press
Charleston, SC 29403
www.historypress.net

Cover Image: Courtsey NOAA
All black-and-white images courtesy of *Coastal Observer* unless otherwise noted.
All color images courtesy NOAA unless otherwise noted.

First published 2006

Manufactured in the United States

ISBN 1.59629.133.8

Library of Congress Cataloging-in-Publication Data

Rubillo, Tom.
A history of hurricane destruction in South Carolina : hell and high water
/ Tom Rubillo.
p. cm.
Includes bibliographical references.
ISBN 1-59629-133-8 (alk. paper)
1. Hurricanes--South Carolina--History. I. Title.
QC945.R83 2006
363.34'92209757--dc22
2006009442

With very special thanks to my wife Claire for all her help in reading, researching and encouraging the writing of this book. Her keen wit, warm companionship and wise perception turned those chores into great fun.

While I love all three of my children deeply and equally, this book is dedicated to my youngest son and very good pal Jeffrey.

Contents

Prologue

We all were sea-swallowed, though some cast again,
And by that destiny to perform an act;
Whereof what's past is prologue, what is to come
In yours and my discharge.
William Shakespeare, *The Tempest*, act 2, scene 1

The following is excerpted from an unsigned letter on the second page of the October 5, 1822 edition of the *Carolina Gazette*.

Debordieu 30ᵗʰ...I am requested to apprise you of the calamitous visitation that has befallen Dr. Myer's family. It has pleased God in the inscrutable wisdom of His decrees to sweep from a numerous remnant of afflicted relations the entire family of Dr. Levy Myers. The house in which the Doctor resided was wrecked and floated away, and with it, himself and every member of his family, fifteen in number...
The loss of lives at North Inlet has been distressingly awful. Whole families were crushed in the general ruin.

Modern-day Debordieu is a gated community in Georgetown, South Carolina. Many of its stately homes are located on or near the beach, the families they shelter imperiled by the sea. North Inlet is a wildlife preserve that borders Debordieu.

*

Of all nature's furies, the most violent and dangerous is the hurricane. The intense swirling winds—clockwise below the equator and counterclockwise above—have, throughout history, killed people, sent ships to the ocean floor, destroyed homes, devastated forests and wildlife and have left suffering in their wake.

The destructive power of hurricanes is directly related to the speed of their winds and the height of the "storm surge." Storm surge is a wall of water pushed ahead of a hurricane's onshore winds. The classification system that has been created to rate hurricanes takes these two physical phenomena into account and provides some advance notice of just how destructive a storm will become.

When wind blowing over the open water causes the seas to become rough, small craft advisories are issued so that casual boaters will not venture out and into harm's way.

When a group of clouds form thunderstorms that circulate in an organized way, the mass is called a tropical depression. A weather system will carry that designation until its winds exceed thirty-eight miles per hour. At that point, meteorologists give special attention to its course, direction and speed. Gale warnings are raised so that ship captains and all boaters can steer clear of choppy waters.

A storm is reclassified as a tropical storm when its maximum sustained winds exceed thirty-eight miles per hour. Aircraft and ships at sea are warned of its presence. Weather forecasters become even more alert, as do the news media in affected areas.

A tropical storm officially becomes a hurricane when its maximum sustained winds reach seventy-five miles per hour. At this point, each system is given a human name. Initially, because of the hurricane's fury, only the names of women were used. Hurricanes being swirling masses of hot air, men's names have been added in recent years.

When it begins to look as if a tropical weather system may become dangerous, specially equipped airplanes fly repeatedly through the storm in each primary direction to measure storm intensity and predict its future path.

Once classified as a hurricane the storm's destructive potential becomes the criteria used to give it a category on the Saffir-Simpson Hurricane Damage Potential Scale.

A category one storm will have maximum sustained winds between 75 and 95 miles per hour. Most wind damage will be to trees and shrubs. Unanchored objects go flying, making it very unwise to be outside. Very low-lying marshes, waterfront and coastal areas flood. The storm surge along the coast caused by storm winds will be between four to five feet above the normal tide. Evacuation routes begin to flood and can become impassable.

A storm grows to category two when its winds are between 96 and 110 miles per hour. At that intensity, the wind begins to damage the roofs, doors and windows of buildings. Trees and shrubs are blown down. Flying debris becomes more dangerous. Mobile homes begin to come apart. Boats are torn from their moorings. Piers suffer damage. The tidal surge of the storm rises to between six and eight feet above the normal tide. At the upper levels of a category two storm, emergency workers are called inside. It is simply too dangerous for anyone to be outside, even first responders. Evacuation from all low-lying areas for a category two storm is highly advisable and probably should be mandatory.

Once a storm reaches category three, it has become very dangerous. Its winds are blowing steadily at somewhere between 111 and 130 miles per hour. Many buildings experience extensive structural damage, particularly older ones erected before building standards were upgraded to account for hurricane winds. Walls and roofs begin to give way. Mobile homes are completely destroyed. Cars are overturned. With a tidal surge between nine and twelve feet above the ordinary tide, flooding becomes much more widespread.

A category four storm is dreadful. With winds between 131 and 155 miles per hour and a storm surge of between thirteen and eighteen feet, even strong buildings come apart. Roofs collapse. Walls cave in. Large old trees crack and fall. Just about everyone within ten miles of the ocean is in danger of death or serious bodily injury.

Category five. Those two words should strike terror into the hearts of every sane person. With winds over 155 miles per hour, the damage caused by a category five storm is catastrophic. Storm surges exceed eighteen feet—over the top of the roofs of any one-story buildings that may still be standing. Taller buildings offer no safety. Foundations and first floors of multi-story buildings are washed away, collapsing their upper floors. God help any remaining inhabitants. Floodwaters spread miles and miles inland all along the coast.

In 1969, Hurricane Camille struck the Mississippi coastline on August 17. It had intensified into a category five storm by the time it hit the Gulf Coast. Its sustained winds approached two hundred miles per hour.

Residents of one beachfront condominium decided to stay and enjoy a "hurricane party" as the storm neared. Almost all of them died when their high-rise building collapsed into the relentlessly surging sea. All but three of them died. One of them was later plucked from a tree some five miles inland. All three survivors were severely traumatized by the experience.

Damage does not necessarily end once a storm has passed. Tidal surges can change the topography of land, seriously erode beaches and wash away barrier islands. But that can be the least of it. Flooding can cause wastewater systems to overflow and otherwise release hazardous chemicals into the environment. Hurricane Katrina provided a stunning example of this sort of long-term damage. Katrina caused massive flooding along the Gulf Coast and in the city of New Orleans in September of 2005. Floodwaters mixed with gasoline in cars, crude oil stored at refineries, chemicals being mixed at area factories and those stored under the sinks and in garages of regular households. The chemical cocktail of toxins spread with floodwaters. Many of the ingredients were left behind in the mud by receding water.

Katrina was not an isolated incident of massive environmental damage caused by a hurricane. In 1999, Hurricane Floyd, a huge and very intense storm, took aim at the southeast coast of the United States, including South Carolina. One of the nation's greatest peacetime evacuations took place. Over two million people fled their homes.[1]

Hurricane Floyd was a near miss for South Carolina. It made landfall just across the border with North Carolina. There, the storm dumped record rains of more than twenty inches in many places.

In North Carolina, floodwaters drowned most of the forty-one people who died in Hurricane Floyd there (out of the total of sixty-eight who died as a result of Floyd in the United States). Floyd left some six thousand people homeless. The storm's waters killed one hundred thousand hogs in North Carolina. Between crops and livestock, our neighbors to the north suffered $1.5 billion in farm losses. In addition, millions of gallons of raw hog feces flowed into area streams and rivers when earthen dams holding that waste became rain-soaked and collapsed. The waste, along with nitrogen, phosphorus, bacteria, viruses, pesticides, heavy metals, ammonia and other contaminants poisoned waterways, both in North Carolina and downstream, killing fish, wildlife and, with the passage of time, people.

Floyd's path of destruction continued to spread as the storm moved up the East Coast. As far north as Philadelphia, floodwaters saturated an unlined landfill adjacent to Darby Creek, a small stream dividing the southwestern border of the city from adjoining Delaware County. Toxins of every imaginable type poured out of the dump into draining water and flooded a huge area, including the Tinicum Wildlife Preserve. From there the heavily contaminated waters flowed into the Delaware River, Delaware Bay and, eventually, the Atlantic Ocean, adding to the pollution levels of each.

Tens of thousands of people live and work in the areas surrounding Darby Creek. Only careful environmental surveys can determine whether the flooded area remains fit for human habitation or is a brownfield in need of reclamation. No such study has been performed. Instead, the potential danger is being ignored.

According to one recent study, some sixty million Americans live in places that are vulnerable to hurricanes. There are as many as 338,000 buildings within 500 feet of the nation's coastline. The Federal Emergency Management Agency (FEMA) estimates that at least 87,000 of these are homes that are immediately threatened by storms. But because 80 or more percent of people who live along the Atlantic have never experienced a hurricane (or, worse, have evacuated only to experience a glancing blow), many have a false sense of security about the danger.

When it comes to hurricanes, an illusion of safety is dangerous. Living in harm's way is one thing. Tarrying in the face of an emerging threat is something else. Even a small delay can prove fatal.

Just one of many examples of the danger of delay can be seen along South Carolina's Grand Strand, the upper sixty miles or so of the northern end of the state's Atlantic coast. It is a long barrier island that is separated by a wide river from the mainland and higher ground.

The Grand Strand is one of the fastest growing and developing areas in the United States. Thousands relocate there every year. Millions of people visit its beaches, golf courses and other attractions each year. While Myrtle Beach is the best known of the various vacation communities, all of them are becoming increasingly popular.

The available evacuation routes at the northern end of the Grand Strand are marginally adequate for the task. The same is not true along the southern end. There, the beaches and attractions of Georgetown County (Garden City Beach, Murrells Inlet, North Litchfield Beach, Litchfield Beach, Pawleys Island and the exclusive communities of Prince George and Debordieu Colony Club) draw increasing numbers of new residents and visitors each year.

The increase in both permanent and seasonal populations notwithstanding, there remains only one evacuation route from these beach communities on the Strand's southern third. It is U.S. Highway

17. At present, that road has two lanes generally headed north and two lanes headed south. The lanes to the north lead to even more congested beach communities and are of no help during an evacuation. The route to the south crosses two high bridges (dipping on a low-lying island in the middle) before entering onto the mainland.

The city of Georgetown lies at the opposite side of the two bridges. Developed in lowlands at the head to Winyah Bay, Georgetown is a charming, tree shaded, old colonial town. The site was chosen by earlier settlers because the waters of five rivers converge there. Because of its proximity to water, almost all of the city of Georgetown is located in a flood zone.

While much attention has been given by city government to drainage projects in recent years, the most serious flood zone from an evacuation standpoint remains ignored. It is along U.S. Highway 17 between Broad and King Streets just a few blocks from the two bridges entering Georgetown. There, Highway 17 traverses a natural bowl in the earth. Storm water drains and pipes there are inadequate. Upgrading them would require a lot of digging through a predominately white, middle-class residential neighborhood. Not noted for their foresight, some local politicians have been unwilling to disturb registered voters in that area. Others are either blind to, or feign ignorance of, the problem.

In an ordinary seasonal heavy rain, the roadway can flood, becoming impassable. Traffic backs up. When this occurs, as it certainly will at some time in the future, in the face of an approaching hurricane, evacuees will end up stranded in their vehicles. That would be dangerous enough, particularly as the water begins to rise. Those still on the high bridges when strong winds hit will be in danger of being blown away while cowering in their cars. Those getting out to run for shelter would likely be blown away, drowned in rising waters, struck by flying debris or meet some similar gruesome fate. If they are lucky enough to reach higher ground (about a half a mile's distance), there is no public shelter awaiting them.

Simply put, the death toll could prove appalling at just this one location. But since this tragedy has not happened so far, those responsible for the public's safety at this location remain oblivious. Readers familiar with local topography elsewhere will likely know of similar dangerous situations in their communities. If Hurricane Katrina taught us anything, it is that neither federal, state nor local authorities are as aware or prepared for danger as they may suppose.

In the twentieth century, around a dozen hurricanes of varying intensity have struck the South Carolina coastline. By comparison, in the nineteenth century nearly three times as many massive storms ravaged the state's coast. Meanwhile, during the modern lull in storm activity, the beach communities of South Carolina have grown enormously. A very substantial proportion of the people now occupying the coast have never experienced a severe hurricane. The danger, of course, is that the expectations of residents of the area are the result of the recent quiescent period and not of the historic record.

What follows is a history of storms along the South Carolina coast. According to the National Hurricane Center,[2] between the outset of the Industrial Revolution in the 1800s and 2004, South Carolina experienced nineteen category one storms, six category two storms, four category three storms and two category four storms. This book discusses those. But it also includes what can be gleaned from the scant records of the fifteenth, sixteenth, seventeenth and eighteenth centuries. Scientific work is just beginning to put together a storm history from pre-Columbian times. That work is described briefly too.

To the extent both available and interesting, this history of tropical disturbances includes actual stories of things that happened to real people. Some are quite frightening. Others are very sad. But they are not over-dramatized. They simply tell of the experiences of those who lived in this place before our time. They are the lessons of history. We either learn from them or suffer the same consequences. As Shakespeare astutely observed, "what's past is prologue."

1.
Storm Formation

"His way is the whirlwind and the storm, and clouds are the dust of his feet."
Nahum 1:3

Hurricanes are thunderstorms that have been nurtured by a special combination of air and water. Ocean water has to be warmer than eighty-one degrees Fahrenheit to fuel a hurricane. The rate of evaporation of water increases as water temperature goes up. When seawater reaches eighty-one degrees, the evaporation rate becomes sufficient to start the cycle of circulation that can result in a hurricane.

The summer sun in the tropics is quite intense and rapidly heats the atmosphere. This warm air rises. As it does, it carries water vapor with it. When that vapor reaches the cooler high altitudes, it condenses and falls as rain. The rain releases the heat that carried the vapors into the atmosphere in the first place. Hot air taking up more space than cold, its release by the rain expands the storm's mass, decreasing the barometric pressure at the surface. When this happens, warm air from outside the storm rushes in at the bottom and a "tropical wave" (a low-pressure zone that travels west over the warm sea[3]) is created. This causes wind. The wind stirs the sea. The result is more evaporation, more rising water vapor, more rain, more released heat, greater expansion of the storm, increasing wind speeds, lowering of barometric pressure and so on.

If not disturbed by strong horizontal winds or wind sheer, this cycle will remain centered and the cyclone will continue to strengthen. Only an intervening physical condition—cold water, high horizontal winds (strong wind sheer) or the storm passing over land—disrupts the process. Otherwise, at the core of this dynamic system winds will continue to pick up speed. The wind will, in turn, churn ocean waves and push the ocean's warm waters ahead (or, actually, on the right hand side of) the storm. Storm surge is created by this driving force.

The intensity of a hurricane depends almost entirely on the amount of heat that is available to feed it. In addition to the presence or absence of countervailing winds, its longevity depends on how long that heat is available. The speed and path of the storm help determine the latter. A slow moving storm front over late summer tropical water that is otherwise undisturbed by a jet stream or other strong wind sheer can quickly become a killer storm. A fast moving weather front being shredded by the jet stream may disrupt a picnic or even prove to be a hazard to travel or navigation, but will likely be survivable.

All of the storms that have caused the death and destruction described in this book were born somewhere between the earth's equator and thirty degrees north latitude of our delicate blue globe. The general circulation patterns of air found in that region are referred to as the tropical easterlies because they move from east to west from sub-Saharan Africa toward the Americas. Above thirty degrees north latitude, the prevailing winds are the westerlies, moving from west to east from the Americas back toward Europe. South Carolina, being centered at approximately thirty-three degrees north latitude, is right in the middle of the turning point of the general wind circulation pattern.

Tropical weather fronts moving toward the Americas from sub-Saharan Africa begin to curve to the north and then east back toward Europe along the South Carolina coastline. Bull's Bay is in the center of this bull's-eye. If slightly off target to the south, a turning big storm can devastate Beaufort, as did Hurricane Gracie in 1959. If a little off target to the north (like Hurricane Hazel in 1954), Pawleys Island, Myrtle Beach and points in between can be washed to sea.

Both the frequency and the intensity of storms are the product of a very complex series of interactions around the earth. One factor believed to play an important role in hurricane frequency is the temperature of surface water in the eastern Pacific Ocean near the equator. Normally the surface temperature of the ocean there is between sixty and seventy degrees Fahrenheit. When the water warms to around eighty degrees—a condition called El Niño—there are more big storms in the Pacific, but fewer in the Atlantic, Gulf of Mexico and the Caribbean Sea. El Niño, it seems, is related to greater horizontal wind sheer on our side of the globe, so that potential storms are more readily blown apart.

When the surface water in the eastern Pacific cools down below fifty-five degrees as a result of an upwelling of cold, deep ocean water along the equator and west coast of South America—a phenomenon referred to as La Niña—the reverse occurs. Wind sheer in the Atlantic, Gulf of Mexico and Caribbean decreases in La Niña conditions. This allows storm systems to consolidate. As a result, the danger of hurricane formation rises in our quadrant of the globe.

Interestingly, in addition to discouraging storm formation in the Atlantic, El Niño in the Pacific also causes problems for people over widely disparate parts of the globe. El Niño causes a "shift in atmospheric and oceanic circulation that…has been blamed for flooding in Peru, mudslides in California and brush fires in Australia," the *New York Times* recently reported.[4] "But El Niño has an impact far beyond the Pacific Rim. In Africa, for example, the risk of drought increases greatly in El Niño years, with corresponding effects on water supplies, food production and, ultimately, the health of the people living there."[5] Mother Nature, it seems, has gathered many different people in the same basket.

Just as global environmental conditions bear on the frequency of storms, different ones affect a storm's intensity. Whether a gathering storm encounters horizontal wind sheer or not is one and has already been mentioned. Water temperature, however, is probably the other most important factor to storm development and, in particular, storm intensity. The warmer ocean water becomes, the more intense a storm passing over it can grow. That is because hurricanes run on hot water.

During the decades of the industrial age, the earth's climate has gotten steadily warmer. This global warming is a well-documented scientific fact. While politicians continue to argue over whether the warming is manmade or part of a natural cycle, when it comes to hurricanes, the cause does not matter; the effect is the same. Hurricanes are nature's way of shedding excess heat in the oceans' waters. As the atmosphere heats up, so do the oceans' waters. As they do, cyclonic activity in the tropics and sub-tropics becomes more intense. As things cool down, fewer storms of lesser intensity result.

With the world's oceans getting warmer and warmer, the forecast is that hurricanes that do form will be increasingly more intense; more destructive. At the same time, El Niño and La Niña conditions in the Pacific will continue to regulate storm frequency.

The phenomenon known as storm surge was mentioned briefly earlier. It is different from, and in addition to, the relentlessly crashing ocean waves of the storm.

The huge waves of a hurricane are caused when strong winds interact with the ocean's surface: The stronger the wind, the bigger the waves. None of that should be a surprise to anyone.

Storm surge, on the other hand, is a distinct danger. It is the result of low surface pressure in the middle of a hurricane. That low pressure causes the ocean's surface to rise inside the storm, much like liquid will rise in a straw when someone sucks on it and reduces the air pressure inside. The higher pressure outside the straw pushes the liquid down all around the straw and forces liquid up inside it. In that way, dynamic equilibrium is maintained.

Storm surge is created in this same way. As this increased water level inside the hurricane is then driven ahead by the storm's forward movement, the hurricane's strong winds rotating from left to right (counterclockwise) drive this rising water toward the shore on the right-hand side of the storm. When the rising water comes in contact with the rising slope of the continental shelf, it is pushed upward even further and storm surge results. Depending on (1) local topography at the point where it strikes land (2) the height of pounding waves created by the wind and (3) the state of the ordinary tide, the storm surge can rush inland for miles, drowning every living thing that either cannot, or will not, get out of its way.

The effects of storm surge on land usually reaches a peak and returns to normal tide level within a period of six to twelve hours. But when a storm is fast moving, the surge can rise and fall in a matter of minutes to an hour. The surge itself can reach heights of twenty to thirty feet above the ordinary tide and is, by itself, very deadly. It has been estimated that 90 percent of all hurricane-related deaths in the United States are caused by it.[6]

As if this all were not enough, hurricanes frequently spawn miniature versions of themselves in the form of waterspouts over the sea and tornadoes on land. While much smaller in size, these very intense whirlwinds can pack an extremely destructive punch. Since their formation and path inside of a hurricane cannot be forecast and forewarning to those in their path is impossible, these fingers of death within the larger storm only add to the peril.

While we are all equal in the eyes of man's law, when it comes to dealing with the laws of man or nature, not everyone has the same amount of common sense. Those who try to understand both and stay out of harm's way are more likely to survive. Those who do not may eliminate themselves from any intelligent design.

2.

Brave New World

They longed for death to end their dreadful suffering.
Christopher Columbus[7]

God created hurricanes along with everything else, so they have been around for a very long time. What has not been available, however, is a written record of them, at least not until Europeans voyaged to this brave new world. That is where this chronicle begins.

Columbus made his way safely to the shores of the West Indies and back in 1492 without running into a hurricane. That is a pretty remarkable fact. He and his men sailed across the Atlantic at the latitudes and at a time of year when they all were most likely to encounter a hurricane. The three tiny ships upon which they ventured were not equipped or likely to survive the full force of a serious hurricane. That his trip to the New World proved successful was entirely serendipitous, at least from the European point of view. Had he and his crew perished, the world would have remained flat a little longer and the history of the western hemisphere would have been somewhat different.

During his second voyage to the West Indies in 1493, Columbus sailed with a fleet of seventeen ships and 1,200 men. That small fleet encountered a four-hour storm on its way to what later became known as Dominica in the Leeward Islands. The storm split sails and broke some spars. While not a hurricane, the storm is noteworthy because the ships came aglow with St. Elmo's fire.[8] Other than this spectacular natural phenomenon, the fleet made safe passage across the Atlantic during the midst of the months that mark the hurricane season.

When he sailed the Atlantic the second time, Columbus stayed for about three years looking for riches. During that time, he and his men ran into and described a severe storm that struck in September of 1494. Whether it was a hurricane or not is a matter of conjecture.

During the late spring and early summer of 1494, Columbus explored the island of Jamaica. He also ventured throughout the entire southern coast of Cuba. He reportedly ran into a squall in May and his fleet encountered another in July; the second storm was worse than the first. His chronicler, Bishop Las Casas, wrote that "among many things that he suffered was a thunder squall so sudden, horrible and perilous that it threw the flagship on her beam-ends."[9]

Returning to the island of Hispaniola in September 1494, Columbus thought he saw something considered to be a very a bad omen: a sea monster. In Columbus's time, sea monsters were considered a sure sign that bad weather was on the way.

Columbus took the prudent course and sought shelter, anchoring his fleet by a small island just off the tip of Hispaniola. The monster-predicted storm struck, but Columbus and his men rode it out in safe anchorage. Little else is known about this experience.[10] But certainly Columbus learned something useful, since he survived tropical storms throughout the remainder of his ventures in the New World.

In 1495, Columbus encountered more dangerous weather. An account of the experience appears in a 1511 work by historian Peter Martyr entitled *The Decades of the New World or West India*. That description says:

> *This same year in the month of June, they say there rose such a boisterous tempest of wind from the SE, as hath not lately been heard of. The violence hereof was such that it plucked up by the roots whatever great trees were within the force thereof. When this whirlwind came to the haven of the city, it beat down to the bottom of the sea three ships which lay at anchor, and broke the cables in sunder: and that (which is the greater marvel) without any storm of roughness of the sea, only turning them three or four times about. The inhabitants also affirm that the same year the sea extended itself further into the land, and rose higher than ever it did before in the memory of many, by the space of a cubit.*
>
> *The people, therefore, muttered among themselves that our nation had troubled the elements, and caused such portentous signs. These tempests of the air (which the Grecians call Tiphones, that is, whirlwinds), they call Furacanes; which they say, do often times chance in this Island: But that*

neither they nor their great grandfathers ever saw such violent and furious Furacanes, that plucked up great trees by the roots: Neither yet such surges and vehement motions of the sea, that so wasted the land.[11]

Whether this weather system was a hurricane or something else (a water spout that sunk ships in the harbor and then moved on land or, perhaps a tsunami) is a matter of some dispute among experts.[12] Whatever it was, it was frightful.

Columbus made a third voyage west from Spain in 1498, sailing from Spain in late May. After stopping in the Canary and Cape Verde Islands, he headed west. Rather than encounter a hurricane, his small fleet ran into the doldrums around eight degrees north latitude.

The wind stopped so suddenly and unexpectedly and the supervening heat was so excessive and immoderate that there was no one who dared go below to look after the casks of wine and water, which burst, snapping the hoops of the pipes; the wheat burned like fire; the bacon and salted meat roasted and putrefied.[13]

The rest of his time during this third voyage to the New World was meteorologically uneventful. The same cannot be said for his command of the situation, since Columbus was taken back to Spain in chains in 1500 to appear before his patrons, Ferdinand and Isabella of Spain.

Stripped of some of his authority, Columbus returned to the New World for the last time in 1502, arriving in Santo Domingo well ahead of the hurricane season. There were many ships in the harbor when he arrived. Thirty of them were packed with slaves and treasure and were set to sail for Spain. "From the hazy appearance of the atmosphere, the direction of high-flying cirrus, and the presence of an ominous southeasterly swell, Columbus sensed an imminent storm."[14] He tried to warn everyone, but the new governor would not listen. The assembled ships set sail.

In less than two days sail from Santo Domingo, just as the laboring fleet rounded the eastern tip of Hispaniola into Mona Passage, an increasing northeast wind caught the ships. Soon they were laboring heavily in the whole gale. So severe did the blow become, probably reaching full hurricane force, that about 20 vessels went to the bottom with all hands and six others were lost but had some survivors...Over 500 men lost their lives needlessly in this failure to heed the reading of the weather signs, and practically all the treasure which had been extracted from the natives with such toil and cruelty went to the bottom.[15]

Of the treasure ships that sailed, the only one that survived was the *Aguja*. It was carrying gold belonging to Columbus. All of the governor's gold was lost.

Meanwhile, Columbus had wanted to ride out the impending storm by staying in port. Governor Don Nicholas de Orvando of the island of Hispaniola would not let him. So Columbus sailed to the south side of the island and anchored where he could get shelter.[16] When the storm struck, the anchor chains of all his ships broke, except that occupied by Columbus himself. Columbus described the scene, "The storm was terrible and on that night the ships were parted from me. Each one of them was reduced to an extremity, expecting nothing save death; each one of them was certain the others were lost."[17]

Columbus, meanwhile, had spared his ship and crew the worst of the danger "by lying close to the shore, like a sage astrologer who foresaw whence the danger must come."[18]

When the storm was over, Santo Domingo was in ruins. Meanwhile, Columbus sailed from his safe haven into the Caribbean in search of more treasure. He spent the autumn along the shores of Central America. When he finally came about in December of 1502, he encountered trouble. He described it thus:

The tempest arose and wearied me so that I knew not where to turn; my old wounds opened up, and for nine days I was as lost without hope of life; eyes never held the seas so high, angry and covered by foam. The wind not only prevented our progress, but offered no opportunity to run behind any headland for shelter; hence we were forced to keep out in this bloody ocean, seething like a pot on a hot fire. Never did the sky look more terrible; for one whole day and night it blazed like a furnace, and the lightning broke forth with such violence that each time I wondered if it had carried off my spars and sails; the flashes came with such fury and frightfulness that we all thought the ships would be blasted. All this time the water never ceased to fall from the sky; I don't say it rained, because it was like another deluge. The people were so worn out that they longed for death to end their dreadful suffering.[19]

The storm concluded and Columbus and his fleet reassembled. Shortly thereafter, they encountered another frightening event. It was "no less dangerous and wonderful. [A] water spout on that Tuesday, December 13th passed between two ships. Had the sailors not dissolved it by reciting the Gospel according to St. John, it would surely have swamped anything it struck; for it raises the water up to the clouds in a column thicker than a water butt, twisting it about like a whirlwind."[20]

Columbus finally departed the New World for the last time in September of 1504. The last trip back to Spain proved to be an adventure. His ship ran into at least one big storm along the way. It occurred on October 29 and broke his main mast into four pieces. That repaired, Columbus encountered a second storm that broke the rigging again. Columbus finally sailed into port on November 17, 1504, fifty-six days after starting home. His fateful voyages were over.

A little more than four centuries later, Girolamo Benzoni wrote his *History of the New World* about a 1565 storm.[21] In it, he provided the first lengthy description of the newly discovered weather phenomenon that today we call a hurricane:

In those days a wondrous and terrible disaster occurred in this country. At sunrise such a horrible, strong wind began that the inhabitants of the island thought they had never seen or heard anything like it before. The raging storm…came with great violence, as if it wanted to split heaven and earth apart from one another, and hurl everything to the ground. All the people were so shocked by the storm of such unheard-of-violence that they believed with fear and horror that death was wholly before their eyes, and that the elements would completely melt, and the last day was surely at hand. Just then it began to thunder and lightning frightfully, and it thundered so cruelly with cracks and crashes, and the lightning flashes came so quickly after one another that the sky seemed to be completely full of fire. Soon after that a thick and dreadful darkness came to the day which was even darker than any night could be, and no person could see the others for the darkness, but rather had to grope and fumble like the blind to find their way. The people were as a whole so despairing because of their great fear that they ran here and there, as if they were senseless and mad, and did not know what they did. Meanwhile the wind blew with such great and terrible force that it ripped many large trees out of the earth by the roots and threw them over. Similarly some large cliffs also fell down from the force with terrible, awful crashes and turmoil, so that many houses and villages were thrown to the ground including many people who stayed in that place. The strong and frightful wind threw some entire houses and capitals including the people from the capital, tore them apart in the air and threw them down to the ground in pieces. This awful weather did such noticeable damage in such a short time that not three ships stood secure in the sea harbor or come through the storm undamaged. For the anchors, even if they were yet strong, were broken apart through the strong force of the wind and all the masts, despite their being new, were crumpled. The ships were blown around by the wind, so that all the people in them were drowned. For the most part the Indians had crawled away and hidden themselves in holes in order to escape such disaster.

No longer living on a flat earth, Europeans were no longer innocent about the awesome power of Mother Nature.

3.

Carolina Cyclones
In the Beginning

June too soon
July stand by
August look out you must
September remember
October, all over

The Spanish were the dominant European power in the New World for the first half-century after Columbus's voyage of discovery. That is not to say that the other Old World sea powers (Portugal, England and France) were not covetous of New World treasures. They obviously were.

Beginning in the middle of the 1500s, the French challenged Spanish dominance in the New World by establishing footholds in both Florida and South Carolina. Religious persecution at home motivated the effort. During the 1500s, France was under the thumb of the Catholic Church. Its Grand Inquisitors were brutally intolerant of any questioning of accepted religious orthodoxy. Accusation of heresy was quickly followed by torture. Those who confessed (most everyone) were given an opportunity to recant. If they refused, they were impaled, hanged or burned at the stake.

The systematic persecution of heretics ultimately led to the massacre of Huguenots by Catholics on St. Bartholomew's day in 1572. Meanwhile, as fundamentalist frenzy grew more intense, many of France's Protestants sought refuge in the New World. There, they encountered the Spanish.

The Spanish first visited and claimed Florida in 1513. Fifteen years later, in 1528, when they sailed around to what is now Tampa Bay, they ran into trouble. This expedition was shipwrecked in a storm that was most probably a hurricane. Only ten of over four hundred crewmembers survived.[22]

As the Spanish were exploring and laying claim to Florida, Protestant refugees from France established two settlements, one at Fort Caroline at the mouth of Saint John's River in Florida and the other at Charlesfort on Parris Island (now in South Carolina).

Upset with the French intrusion into land claimed for Spain, Admiral Pedro Menendez de Aviles mounted an assault on Fort Caroline. His armada of eleven ships sailed into a hurricane. Only five ships survived. He withdrew his decimated fleet.

Emboldened by the hasty Spanish retreat, the French decided to counterattack. Four hundred Frenchmen set sail on September 19, 1565, to oust the Spanish from their redoubt. Unfortunately, the French also encountered a hurricane and ended up having to make their way back to Fort Caroline on foot. The Spanish, in the meantime, had outmaneuvered the French and taken Fort Caroline. On their return, the French found that the Spanish were inside the fort. The French promptly surrendered on a promise that their lives would be spared. They were not.[23] Meanwhile, without a military to their south to protect them from the Spanish, the French settlement at Parris Island failed.

Attempts by the English to colonize the New World encountered nature's wrath too. In 1584, Sir Walter Raleigh led an expedition to Albemarle Sound (now part of North Carolina) and named the entire area Virginia. This name for a much wider stretch of the mid-Atlantic coast can create some confusion when looking at the historical record. In any event, in 1585, a small group of Englishmen abandoned their settlement after experiencing an extremely severe storm that was probably a hurricane.

The very next year, 1586, Sir Francis Drake sailed into the area, but left shortly after because "there arose a great storm (which they said was extraordinary and very strange) and lasted three days together, and put our fleet in great danger."[24] As described by one colonist, "The 13th of June our ships were forced to put to sea. The weather was so sore and the storm so great that our anchors would not hold…And our ship the Primrose broke an anchor of 250 lbs. weight. All the time we were in this country we had thunder and rain with hailstones as big as hen's eggs. There were great spouts at the seas as though heaven and earth would have met."[25]

In 1587, Drake returned to the settlement he had tried to establish the year before. The fifteen men he had left behind to guard the place were gone. Shortly after his arrival, "there arose such a tempest at northeast that our Admiral [Drake] then riding out of the harbor, was forced to cut his cables and put to sea, where he lay beating off and on six days before he could come to us again."[26]

The leaders of this attempt at colonization departed for England for more supplies, leaving another small group behind. The war between England and Spain that was otherwise raging at the time (including the sinking of the Spanish armada at Cadiz in 1588) prevented a return trip until 1590. Upon their return in August of that year, the supply ships ran into two storms, reporting "We had very foul weather, with much rain, thundering and great spouts, which fell around us, high unto our ships."[27] But by this time the colony at Roanoke—Lorna Donne and all—had mysteriously disappeared into the annals of history.

In his definitive work *Early History of Hurricanes, 1492-1870*, David Ludlum reported that:

> *a final expedition visited the Carolina shore in August 1591 and once again had to contend with a strong northeast gale on the 16th. "For at this time the wind blew at northeast and direct into the harbor so great a gale, that the sea broke extremely on the bar, and the tide went very forcibly at the entrance." Out of the broad Atlantic no less than four destructive storms occurred in the four weeks from 10 August to 6 September 1591, with the destruction of at least 27 ships reported. The Grand Fleet making its annual treasure run from Havana to Old Spain was caught in the 10 August gale and over 500 sailors went to the bottom with most of their loot.*[28]

From the fragmentary written record that is available, it appears that at least a dozen storms occurred in the latter part of the sixteenth century, which had at least an indirect effect on the early history of the European occupation of the Carolinas.

4.
Seventeenth-Century Storms

When Charles II issued a land grant to eight Lord Proprietors in 1665, the colony of Carolina was bounded to the north by what today is called Virginia and by the middle of the Florida peninsula to the south.[29] The grant included all the land between the Atlantic and Pacific Oceans. These boundaries were later modified. As with Virginia in the previous century, boundaries were different from those today. So, once again, deciding exactly where certain storms of early colonial times made landfall can prove to be tricky business. But the written record from the times are a little better, making the history of seventeenth century storms striking South Carolina a little clearer.

"The Dreadful Hurry Cane" of 1667

From the time they first came to what is now South Carolina, English settlers had to be mindful of the sea. It was their only link to the other English-speaking civilization upon which they were so dependent for re-supply. The sea also was the most likely route by which potential rival Europeans, the Spanish in particular, might invade them. A few years after their arrival, they learned of another danger.

William Bartram was America's first botanist. His home and gardens were on the banks of the Schuylkill River, the largest tributary feeding the Delaware River in Philadelphia. He was a friend and contemporary of Benjamin Franklin.

Bartram toured the Carolinas and documented flora unique to the area in 1765 and 1766. Part of his journal records accounts of hurricanes from the preceding one hundred years. One of his accounts relates to the storm before the English arrived. Bartram reported that "the Indians told the English that they know one that raised the water over the tops of the trees where the town [of Charleston] now stands."[30]

Hurricane chronicler David Ludlum speculates that this storm—the one recounted by the Indians that occurred before the settlers arrived—was the same one that ravaged the eastern seaboard in 1667. Known as "The Dreadful Hurry Cane, " an account of it appeared in a pamphlet published in London sometime around the end of that same year. It reported:

Having this opportunity, I cannot but acquaint you with the relation of a very strange tempest which hath been in the parts (with us called a hurricane) which began August 27 and continued with such violence, that it overturned many houses, burying in the ruins much goods and many people, beating to the ground such as were any wares employed in the fields, blowing many cattle that were near the sea or rivers into them, whereby unknown numbers have perished, to the great affliction of all people, few having escaped who have not suffered in their persons or estates, much corn was blown away, and great quantities of tobacco have been lost, to the great damage of many and the utter undoing of others. Neither did it end here, but the trees were torn up by the roots, and in many places whole woods blown down, so that they cannot go from plantation to plantation. The sea (by the violence of the winds) swelled twelve foot above its usual height, drown the whole country before it, with many of the inhabitants, their cattle and goods, the rest being forced to save themselves in the mountains nearest adjoining, where they were forced to remain many days together in great want, till the violence of the tempest was over, which while it continued, was accompanied with a very violent rain that continued twelve days and nights together without ceasing, with that fury, that none were able to stir from their shelters, though almost famished for want to provisions. The ships that were in the rivers have sustained great damage, but we hope there is none of them lost. This tempest, for the time, was furious that it hath made a great desolation, overturning many plantations, so there was nothing that could stand its fury. We are now with all the industry imaginable repairing our shattered houses, and gathering together what the tempest hath left us. Although it was not alike violent in all places, yet there is scarce any place in the whole country where there is not left sufficient marks of its ruins…

Such hurricanes on the land are seldom heard of, but hurricanes upon the sea are common in these parts, which are many times very prejudicial

Hurricane Hugo
NOAA-11
AVHRR HRPT (1KM)
Multi-spectral False Color Image
September 21, 1989 @ 1844 UTC

1. Hugo looms.

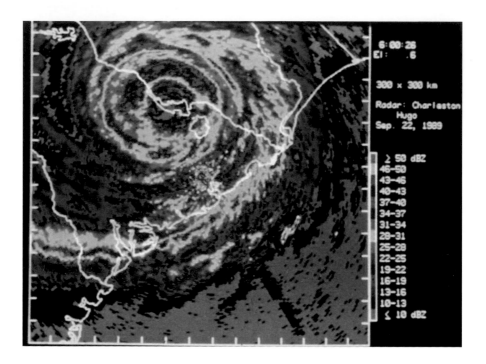

2. Hugo caused damage far inland.

3. Size doesn't matter, intensity does.

4. Hugo ripped away almost half of this home on Folly Beach. *Photo courtesy* The News and Courier/The Evening Post.

5. Destruction in Garden City.

6. Exterior damage to the Holiday Inn at Myrtle Beach.

7. Hugo damaged these mobile and manufactured homes at Surfside Beach.

8. A house on the southern tip of Charleston fared well during Hugo, but the car was not so lucky.

9. Isaac Rivers, 72, waits for his nephew to help collect some of his belongings from what was his Awendaw home. *Photo courtesy* The News and Courier/The Evening Post.

10. Beach houses in Garden City were carried away by Hugo. *Photo courtesy of the* Georgetown Times.

11. Pawleys Island creek cuts a new channel at homeowner's expense. *Photo courtesy of the* Georgetown Times.

and dangerous to the ships trading here. It was by a hurricane that excellent Command Lord Willoughby perished, with divers others in his company. By these kinds of tempests the King of Spain hath lost at several times near 1,000 sail of ships.

In a letter about the "dreadful Hurry Cane," Thomas Ludwell wrote to a Lord Berkeley that people whose homes were near rivers and creeks were "forced to climb to the top of their houses to keep themselves above water." He lamented that "the night of it was the most dismal time I ever knew or heard of, for the wind and rain raised so confused a noise, mixed with the continual cracks of falling houses" in colonial America.[31]

The "grievous hurricane" of 1686 that saved Charleston

The second storm recounted by William Bartram was that of 1686. As the acts of man, fate and fortune would have things, by the mid-1680s Spanish colonists in St. Augustine, Florida, were very upset with their British neighbors to the north. In the preceding one hundred or so years, the Spanish had ousted the French from Florida. With ambitions for more land to the north, they eyed the Carolinas with envy.

Local lure in Georgetown County has it that Vasquez de Ayllon had attempted to establish a settlement in Winyah Bay along South Carolina's northern coastline in 1526 while, simultaneously, Ponce de Leon was scouring Florida looking for the fountain of youth. No archaeological evidence of de Ayllon's foray into South Carolina has been found. Ponce de Leon died. From these two facts it can be confidently stated that neither of these Spanish ventures proved successful. Nonetheless, the Spanish continued to maintain their hold on Florida.

Time elapsed, and as it did, English and Scottish settlers began their conquest and occupation of the South Carolina Lowcountry. This effort began in the mid-1600s. As it turned out, the immigrants from the British Isles were not good neighbors to either the Spanish or the indigenous population.

John Stuart had organized a group of Scots colonists in what he modestly named "Stuart Town" near present-day Beaufort. In March of 1686 he and some of his fellows raided Spanish settlements near St. Augustine, Florida. During that foray, the Scots captured twenty-two slaves, burned several towns, menaced a mission and killed fifty Timucuan Indians.[32]

The raid had not been approved by the English governor (there was a good bit of conflict between the Scots and the English at the time). This

British political distinction mattered little to the Spanish. All Anglos were the same as far as they were concerned. So the Spanish planned a retaliatory attack on the Scots in Stuart Town and the English around Edisto Island and in Charleston for late August or early September (August on the Julian calendar; September on the Gregorian) of 1686.[33]

Three Spanish ships sailed into Port Royal with one hundred Spanish soldiers and additional Indian support fighters under the command of Spanish General Thomas De Leon. Stuart Town was ravaged by disease at the time and there were only about thirty men capable of putting up any sort of defense. The surprise attack routed the defenders. Stuartonians took to the woods. Left without interference, the invaders pillaged and plundered Stuart Town before burning it to the ground.

The Spanish then sailed north.[34] They ransacked isolated plantations on the Edisto River, stole slaves and killed the brother-in-law of the governor. Fortunately for the people of Charleston, a "dreadful hurry cane" struck the South Carolina coast as the Spanish raiders sailed from Edisto toward Charleston. De Leon's flagship, the *Rosario*, was grounded. De Leon drowned. A second ship was beached and burned. Only the remaining third ship escaped back to St. Augustine.[35]

In an unsigned letter to the Lord Proprietors in London, a storm survivor wrote:

> As the night came exceeding black and menacing clouds began to show themselves and were the next morning succeeded by a hurricane wonderfully horrid and destructive whereof your Lordships shall hereafter receive a more particular relation...
>
> The whole country seems to be one entire map of devastation. The greatest part of our houses are blown down and still lie in their ruin, many of us do not have the least cottage to secure us from the rigor of the weather. The long incessant rains have destroyed almost all our goods which lie entombed in the ruins of our houses. Our corn is all beaten down and by means of continued wet weather lies rotting on the ground...
>
> [A]ll over the country...most of our cattle are in great danger of running wild, there being scarce any probability of finding them or possibility of driving them home when they are found...
>
> With the falls of trees the food of our hogs is likewise destroyed which will cause them all to run wild; or which is as bad, they will all be starved from these and the like calamities which now attend us. We have too great

reason to fear the near approach of famine to complete all our miseries which we pray God in his mercy to direct from us.

And now having given your Lordships a brief account of the invasion of the land by the Spaniards, a cruel and inveterate enemy, and the inconceivable detriment we have sustained by the terrible hurricane, we crave leave to acquaint your Lordships with the sad consequences thereof both at present and what we may reasonably expect for the future.[36]

Charleston had been savaged by storm. But it was spared the ravages of the Spanish Conquistadors. While devastating to homes, foodstuffs and livestock, the storm did not result in a massacre or require its survivors to learn a new language.

Local history tells of one additional benefit from this storm.[37] In its aftermath, a battered brigantine put in at Charleston harbor for repairs. The ship's cargo included rice from Madagascar. While in port, the ship's captain, John Thurber, gave a basket of rice to planter Dr. Henry Woodward. Woodward planted the seed. His crop flourished and he shared the seed with other Lowcountry settlers.

Within a few years the rice known as Carolina Gold was being marketed. A labor-intensive crop, local planters fulfilled their desire for bigger and bigger yields by enslaving others. The "rice culture" was born. It thrived until 1865, when planters were stripped of their power to keep others in bondage. That change in labor-management relations curtailed the industry. The death knell to rice as a profitable crop in South Carolina tolled from 1893 to 1911 when hurricanes devastated remaining rice fields. But more about those storms will appear later in this book.

"The Hurricane of the Rising Sun"

Depending on whose version of events is more accurate, the Carolina coast suffered its next major natural disaster in either 1699[38] or 1700.[39] Being so long ago, the year does not matter that much. What is important is what happened to the people who experienced the disaster.

The Scottish ships the *Rising Sun*, the *Duke of Hamilton* and several smaller ships were anchored outside of Charleston harbor. Because of their size, the ships could not safely navigate across a bar at the entrance to the port's haven.

This small fleet was en route from Panama back to Scotland. It was carrying the survivors of an abortive attempt to establish a settlement along the steamy, malarial coast of Central America. The fleet had stopped at Charleston to take on fresh water and other supplies before venturing into the Atlantic for its final leg home.

A small party from this refugee fleet went ashore. While they were there, a powerful hurricane struck, driving the sea before it. Charleston's wharves were washed away. The town was flooded and the people sought refuge on their rooftops.[40] Meanwhile, the wind and water drove the *Rising Sun* onto the shore where it was smashed by the relentless surf. Captain James Gibson and everyone still on board were killed. Close to one hundred souls perished. Their bodies washed ashore and were found along James Island. They were all buried there.

A letter to the Lords of the Admiralty dated in October 1700 read as follows:

> *Some Scotchmen are newly arrived hither from Carolina that belonged to the ship Rising Sun (the biggest ship they sent out for the Caledonia expedition) who tell me that on the third of last month a hurricane happened on that coast, as the ship lay an anchor, within less than three leagues of Charles Town in Carolina with another Scotch ship called the Duke of Hamilton and three or four other; that the ships were all shattered in pieces and all the people lost, and not a man saved. The Rising Sun had 112 men on board. The Scotchmen that are come hither say that 15 of 'em went on shore before the storm to buy fresh provisions at Charleston Town by which means they were saved. The other of their ships they suppose were lost in the Gulf of Florida in the same storm.*[41]

The storm had other victims too. The native people along the coast suffered greatly after the arrival of the English in the Carolinas. Once numerous, smallpox and other diseases spread by the newcomers took a heavy toll on the aboriginal population. So did the slave trade. The Lord Proprietors had given permission to the settlers to capture and sell coastal tribesmen into slavery. This practice also decimated the natives. Those that were unfortunate enough to be captured were shipped to the West Indies and sold into a life of drudgery, disease and death. The tribes around Winyah Bay (the Santee, the Winyah and, to a lesser extent because of their remoteness from foreign settlers, the Pee Dee) in what is now Georgetown County were particular targets for this sort of exploitation. Meanwhile, both the settlers and the Lord Proprietors profited from the trade—settlers reaping profits from the sales and the Lord Proprietors collecting a twenty-shilling tax on each slave that was exported.[42]

Unable to communicate with fellow tribesmen who were captured and shipped away, remaining Indians did not know the full horror that awaited those that had been taken captive. Nonetheless, because of the way they were being treated by the newcomers to their lands, native people became suspicious that they were being cheated. Seeing the furs they traded being loaded on ships, members of the Seewee tribe decided to find out for themselves what was going on. Loading large canoes with their skins and other trade goods, they set sail in the Atlantic in the hope of following the white man's ships.

Those who ventured out to sea were caught in the same storm that sunk the *Rising Sun*. Tribesmen who did not drown were picked up by passing ships. Those who drowned were the lucky ones. The survivors were sold into slavery in the West Indies.[43]

5.

Eighteenth-Century Storms

Even the winds and the waves obey him.
Matthew 8:27

The eighteenth century had an auspicious beginning in Charleston. Spanish influence in the New World had begun to wane by 1700. Pirates who had previously preyed on ships filled with gold from the Caribbean and Central America had fallen on hard times. The Spanish had already stolen most of the treasure amassed by the native peoples, so galleons worth looting were sailing less often. To earn a living, pirates had to adapt to changing economic conditions. They did this by moving up the coast of North America, attacking and pillaging whatever targets of opportunity became available.

One group of these new entrepreneurs was "a motley crew of Portuguese, French, English and Indians" whose homeport was in Havana. They patrolled the waters around Charleston. This "motley crew" was successful enough to result in crewmembers bickering about how to divide their profits. Their dispute was ultimately resolved by majority vote, with the disgruntled minority shareholders (a group of nine English pirates) being set adrift in a longboat. After a brief adventure at sea, the outcast buccaneers made landfall near Charleston.

The truth of their situation being insufficient for their purposes, the Englishmen told rescuers that they were honest seamen whose appearance was the result of their being the few survivors of a harrowing shipwreck. Sympathetic rescuers gave them shelter. This Southern hospitality was short-lived. As it turned out, the captains of three of the ships the pirates had plundered were still in port. The officers recognized the marooned pretenders and disclosed their true occupation. A fair trial preceded their hanging. Charleston was becoming a respectable port of call.[44] This newfound genteel quality would be tested over the next century by a dozen storms.

The storm of 1713

Seventy people died on September 5–6, 1713, along the Carolina coast.[45] During those two days a savage wind "raged so furiously that it drove the sea into Charles-town, damaging much of the fortifications whose resistance it is thought preserved the town. Some low situated houses not far from the sea were undermined and carried away with the inhabitants; ships were drove from their anchors far within land, particularly a sloop... was drove three miles over marshes into the woods."[46]

From available accounts, it appears that the eye of the storm made landfall around Charleston or a little north of the colonial town. Port Royal to the southwest of Charleston barely felt its effects.

The few surviving eyewitness accounts of the storm are vivid. Thomas Lamboll wrote that

> On September 5th came on a great hurricane, which was attended by such an inundation from the sea, and to such an unknown height that a great many lives were lost; all the vessels in Charleston harbor except one were driven ashore. The new lookout on Sullivan's Island, of wood, built eight square and eighty feet high, blown down; all the front wall and mud parapet before Charleston undermined and washed away, with the platform and gun carriages, and other desolations sustained as never before happened in this town. To the northward of Charleston the hurricane was more violent.[47]

Dr. Francis Le Jau thought that it was "miraculous how any of us came to escape from the great Hurricane." He reported that the storm lasted twelve hours and that the Ashley and Cooper rivers "joined for some time." Seventy people drowned in Charleston and houses, barns and plantations were destroyed according to him. "God in his Goodness has preserved us," he wrote.[48]

The deluge of 1722

In mid-September 1722, a large storm struck New Orleans, Louisiana. Forty-four houses, a church, its parsonage and a hospital were destroyed. As in Hurricane Katrina in 2005, many hospital patients were injured. Ships were torn from their moorings; small boats and launches sank or were grounded.[49]

The effects of this storm were felt throughout the southeast. After losing momentum once it struck the Gulf Coast, the Louisiana storm cast its huge umbrella of moisture as it moved northeast, causing huge amounts of rain, including in Charles Town. The storm was so memorable that some forty years later area residents told William Bartram about it. He wrote

> *In the year 1722 in September was the most violent rain for 3 days and 3 nights without intermission that the English inhabitants ever knew. It so flowed in the country as to cause great destruction of grain and other necessaries of life. It seemed as if the collection of vapors that used periodically to operate in currents of wind was discarded in rain.*[50]

Elsewhere, another chronicler, discussing the same storm, wrote

> *About the middle of September here fell the greatest flood attended with a hurricane that has been known since the country was settled. Great numbers of cattle, horses, hogs and some people were drowned. The deer were found frequently lodged on high trees. The wind was so violent that it tore up by the roots great numbers of trees, and disrobed others of their leaves, cones and seed.*[51]

These descriptions help illustrate an important point about cyclonic weather systems. Their devastation is not isolated or reserved to the target struck by the storm's eye. The effects can be very widespread. In the case of this storm, its probable path had carried it over Port Royal, Jamaica, on September 8, causing great loss of life before wandering across the Gulf of Mexico, striking New Orleans and then crossing over the South Atlantic colonies.[52]

The hurricane of 1728

The next major blow to the fledgling colony of South Carolina came in August of 1728. William Bartram wrote that in early August

*We had a very violent hurricane, the wind being north-northeast and
continuing from north-northeast to east-northeast for about six hours,
from nine o'clock in the morning to three in the afternoon; and as the
tide began to ebb the wind shifted to the southeast and east-southeast, still
blowing violently until four of the clock on Saturday morning; at which
time it began to thunder, attended with violent showers of rain, and then
it broke up. But the wind continued at southeast, or thereabouts, for
several days after.*[53]

Some eight ships were lost, along with 1,531 barrels of rice. Another fifteen
ships were damaged in this storm. Two men-of-war that were stationed in
the area to protect shipping from piracy, the *Fox* and the *Garland*, successfully
rode out of the storm at sea. Also according to a news account from the *Boston
Weekly Letter* of October 24, 1728, the fury "hath done a vast deal of damage
on the land to the houses, wharfs and bridges, besides the destroying [of an]
abundance of corn, and other fruits of the earth." The same story reported
that "[s]everal lives were lost, both White men and Negroes."

As far as can be ascertained from the scant accounts available, this storm
was not felt one hundred miles inland. Instead, it was primarily a coastal
storm that wended its way up the Carolina coast.

Benjamin Franklin's storm of 1743 and the birth of a new science

No history of hurricanes can be deemed complete without mention of the
storm of late October 1743. While it did not strike South Carolina, its long-
lasting meteorological effects still have their impact in the modern world.

There was a lunar eclipse visible in the American colonies during the
evening of October 21, 1743. Among the people interested in observing
it was America's first true scientist, Benjamin Franklin. Unfortunately, he
was prevented from making observations by a violent storm that struck
Philadelphia.

Disappointed, Franklin returned to his numerous intellectual and other
pursuits. Then he read the following account in the *Boston Evening Post* of
October 24, which said

*Last Friday night, soon after a total and visible eclipse of the Moon
(which began about nine and ended past one o'clock) came on a storm
of wind and rain, which continued all the following day with great*

41

violence, and the wind being at northeast, the tide was raised as high within a few inches, as that remarkable one about 20 years ago: And as Dr. Ames had given no hint in his almanac of these events, (for which omissions let him answer) which might have put the people on guard, the greatest damages by far has been done here, that was ever known to be done by a storm in the memory of man.

The ever-astute Franklin wrote to his brother for confirmation of the time that the storm had struck Boston. Taking note of the time difference between the storm that had obscured his view of the eclipse in Philadelphia and the time the storm struck Boston, he plotted the storm's probable course and speed. He then made additional inquiries about the timing of other storms upon and down the East Coast.[54]

No one prior to this time had any idea of how or where hurricanes formed, how to track them or, indeed, had even noted the difference between a storm's forward motion and its internal wind circulation. No one, that is, until Benjamin Franklin.

In 1750, Franklin wrote to his friend, Jared Eliot, and postulated a "very singular opinion that, though the course of the wind is from the northeast to the southwest, yet the course of the storm is from the southwest to the northeast." From the information he had garnered relating to the 1743 storm and others, he concluded that rising air that originated and was heated in the south created low pressure which, in turn, drew wind from the north, all of which propelled the coastal storms along a generally north or northeastern track.

Benjamin Franklin's observations, coupled with the historical data later compiled by Philadelphia botanist William Bartram, represent the very beginnings of the science of meteorology. Franklin's later charting of the Gulf Stream during voyages to England and France on behalf of the fledgling republic was his second important contribution to the new science.

The great and deadly hurricanes of 1752

Returning to death and destruction in South Carolina, the next major storm to strike occurred on September 15, 1752. It was the nightmare storm for the Holy City, for it hit Charleston harbor squarely and on the incoming tide. The *South Carolina Gazette* of September 19 described events this way:

The most violent and terrible hurricane that ever was felt in this province, happened on Friday the 15th instant in the morning; and has reduced this Town to a very melancholy situation. As the public doubtless will expect a particular account from the press, we have endeavored to obtain the best information we possibly could of this deplorable calamity; for it is impossible, as yet, to tell all the damage and devastation we have sustained from the violence of the wind and waves.

On the 14th in the evening, it began to blow very hard, the wind being at northeast and the sky looked wild and threatening. It continued blowing from the same point, with little variation, 'till about 4 o'clock in the morning of the 15th, at which time it became more violent, and rained, increasing fast 'till about 9, when the flood came in like a bore, filling the harbor in a few minutes. Before 11 o'clock, all the vessels in the harbor were on shore, except the Hornet man-of-war, which rode it out by cutting away her main mast. All the wharves and bridges were ruined; every house, store &c. upon them beaten down, and carried away (with all the goods, &c. therein), as were also many houses in the town; and abundance of roofs, chimneys, &c. almost all the tiled or slated houses were uncovered; and great quantities of merchandize &c. in the stores on Bay Street damaged, by their doors being burst open.

The town was likewise over-flowed, the tide or sea having rose upwards of 10 feet above the high-water mark at spring tides, and nothing was now to be seen but ruins of houses, canows, wrecks of pettiauguas and boats, masts, yeards, incredible quantities of all sorts of timber, barrels, staves, shingles, household and other goods, floating and driving, with great violence, thro' the streets and round about the town. The inhabitants finding themselves in the midst of a tempestuous sea, the wind still continuing, the tide (according to its common course) being expected to flow 'till after one o'clock, and many of the people already being up to their necks in water in their houses; began now to think of nothing but certain death. But, (Here we must record as signal an instance of the immediate interposition of Divine Providence, as ever appeared), they were soon delivered from their apprehensions; for about 10 minutes after 11 o'clock, the wind veered to the east-southeast, south, and southwest very quick, and then (tho' it continued its violence, and the sea beat and dashed everywhere with amazing impetuosity) the waters fell about 5 feet in a space of 10 minutes, without which unexpected and sudden fall, every house and inhabitant in this town, must, in all probability, have perished. And before 3 o'clock the hurricane was entirely over. Many people were drowned and others much hurt by the fall of houses.

At Sullivan's Island, the pest-house was carried away, and of 15 people that were there 9 were lost, the rest saved themselves by adhering strongly to some of the rafters of the house when it fell, upon which they were driven some miles beyond the island to Hobcaw. At Fort Johnson, the barracks were beat down, most of the guns dismounted, and their carriages carried away. At Craven's and Granville's bastions and the batteries around this town, the cannon were likewise dismounted...

For about 30 miles around Charles-Town, there is hardly a plantation that has not lost every out-house upon it. All our roads are so filled with trees blown and broken down that traveling is rendered extremely difficult; and hardly a fence was left standing in the town or country. Our loss in fine timber trees is almost incredible; and we have suffered greatly also, in the loss of cattle, sheep, hogs, and all kinds of provisions.[55]

Half of the rice crop was lost. Bridges and roads were washed away.[56]

According to the listing of the deadliest Atlantic tropical cyclones between 1492 and 1996 published by the National Oceanic and Atmospheric Administration of the federal government, 103 South Carolinians lost their lives in this storm.

This mid-September storm was quite compact and had little effect on the ports of Georgetown to the north or Port Royal to the south. Georgetown, however, did not escape the fury of the tropics entirely during this hurricane season. For on September 30, 1752, as Charleston was cleaning up from the natural disaster which struck them two weeks earlier, a second storm struck.

The October 3, 1752 edition of the *South Carolina Gazette* carried the following account:

On Saturday last we had here another terrible hurricane, which began with wind and rain at 4 o'clock in the afternoon, but cleared soon after 7 in the evening. For 2 or 3 hours before, the violence of the wind (which blew northeast and at last settled at southeast), and the great quantity of rain that had fallen kept the tides from ebbing their due course and time, so that when this hurricane began to abate, tho' the water should have been low, it was higher than at common spring tides; and had the wind rose as expected, when the flood should have come in, our situation would have been most deplorable indeed! In the town it did little other damage than to the goods of those people who removed from the most exposed places, and the tops of some houses.

But at Winyah [Georgetown to the north] we are informed it was [more] severely felt than the former. About midnight the wind veered around to the northwest when another violent storm broke up the bad weather.

This brief notation of "another violent storm" is somewhat mysterious, but may indicate that the second storm of September to strike South Carolina collided with still another tropical storm that was brewing off the North Carolina coast.

These events occurred one day after the change from the Julian to the Gregorian calendars.[57]

Glancing blows

A storm billed in some accounts as one of the worst of the eighteenth century swept through the West Indies, the Bahamas and offshore of South Carolina in early September 1769. While the wind rose along the coast, it was not severe enough to damage the ripening rice crop. Still, many ships at sea were reported to have lost their masts in the wind. The storm made landfall in North Carolina[58] where it caused very severe damage.

The next significant storm to brush by South Carolina occurred just at the outset of the War for Independence. On August 25, 1775, a storm struck Martinique. Two days later it struck Santo Domingo. After narrowly missing Charleston and the rest of South Carolina's coast, it rammed into North Carolina, killing 163 people. Thereafter, it ran like an express train along the eastern seaboard, leaving great damage in its path. In Virginia, "most of the mill dams…broke, the corn laid almost level with the ground, and fodder destroyed; many ships and others drove ashore and damaged at Norfolk, Hampton, and York."[59] After crossing the Chesapeake Bay, the storm made its way up the Delaware River Valley. In Philadelphia, the river was driven to the highest tides in recorded history there.

The third near miss took place in August of 1778. The fateful storm— one that thwarted a naval battle between the English and French off Rhode Island during the War for Independence—was first recorded as a gale on August 10 over Charleston. Its damage was confined mostly to ships in the harbor and trees and fences being blown over.

The storm came ashore north of Georgetown, sparing that community from serious damage by passage of the weaker left side of the storm over the town. Apparently a very large storm, when it struck New Bern, North Carolina, its winds could still be felt blowing out of the northwest in Charleston well over one hundred miles to the south.[60]

The Occupation Storm of 1781, a night of increasing violence

The city of Charleston had come under siege from both land and sea during the War for Independence. Promises of reinforcement from the Congress were largely unkept. Defenders of the Lowcountry were insufficient in numbers and undersupplied and could not ward off a determined assault by superior numbers. Thus the beloved city of Charleston was left vulnerable to assault by the British.

In 1780, Sir Henry Clinton landed with a force of 11,000 some thirty miles south of Charleston. His month-long land seize, along with a blockade of the port, ultimately resulted in the fall of the city. Governor John Rutledge and his government evacuated in April. On May 12, 1780, the city surrendered. More than 5,500 troops of the Continental Army were disarmed.

When the British took over, they changed the name of the local newspaper to the *Royal Gazette*. It contained largely British propaganda, but it also published meteorological information. Among that scientific data of interest to the local community was the following that appeared on September 5, 1781:

> *The long period of dry weather we lately had, has been followed by a severe storm. On Thursday evening (9 Aug.) about 7 o'clock the wind began to blow from the northeast. Between 8 & 9 it blew fresh, accompanied by rain. It continued to rain and blow from the same quarter with increasing violence during the whole night and yesterday, till one o'clock when the wind shifted to east-northeast. The gale continued to increase till 4 p.m. when the wind having got around to southeast, it blew a mere hurricane. The rain increasing at 8 o'clock the wind began to fall; at high water, 3 o'clock this morning, the storm abated. The wind has now got around to south-southwest but still blows fresh.*

The British ship *Thetis* and the ship *London* sank next to the docks where they were moored. The *London* was later raised. Other ships were driven ashore but re-floated shortly after the storm. The storm had not been severe enough to drive out the British or their sympathizers, some of whom are reported to still reside in Charleston.

The small storm of 1783

On October 7–8, 1783, Charleston was struck by what, according to the damage descriptions, was a category one storm. Its winds began by blowing from the northeast. They continued throughout the day, increasing steadily the whole time. By the next morning it was raining very hard and the wind had increased enough to cause ships to bang into wharves, damaging both. While rising water caused concern initially, a shift in the wind to the northwest "kept the tide down." Had it not done so, the *South Carolina Weekly Gazette* observed when writing of the storm on October 11, "in all probability the city would have experienced all the horrors and destruction of September 1752."

Little damage was done to crops by this storm since the harvest was almost over by the time it struck. Ships that had ridden the storm out at sea suffered little damage.

Sadly, the ship *John & Nelly Bailey* sailed from New York to Charleston on September 22, apparently foundered in the storm and was not heard of after. All aboard the ship perished.

The October storm of 1792

According to an account in the *Charleston Daily Advertiser* of November 2, 1792 and later reprinted elsewhere,

> On Tuesday last (30 Oct) a great quantity of rain fell in this city, attended by very high wind. In the evening the wind increased, and continued to blow with great violence the greatest part of the night. A quarter before 12 o'clock p.m., the wind was due north—at three quarters after 12, it had shifted to east-northeast—at half past one, to southeast—at a quarter past two, to due east—and at three quarters after three, to southeast at which time it blew a severe gale. At four it veered, and got around again to due north.
>
> Considerable damage was done to the wharves and shipping in the harbor…Several small buildings were unroofed and thrown down, and a number of fences leveled with the ground. Some of the inhabitants were apprehensive of an inundation, but it being ebb tide, and the wind shifting to the northwest, prevented this calamity.

Yet another press account described the storm as "one of the heaviest gales it has been felt this many years." In addition to damage to roofs and fences, it reported that "one or two buildings were blown down" and that "most of the vessels in the harbor [were] more or less injured; and two small ones sunk."[61]

While from the description of the damage this was likely a category two or three storm by today's measure, Charleston managed to dodge the bullet because the storm struck on a falling tide.

October 1797

As the century was coming to a close, Charleston experienced another near miss. In mid-October, a storm that had formed in the Caribbean crossed over Cuba, passed between the Bahamas and Florida and traveled along the coast of Georgia. As it passed, numerous ships found themselves grounded on Florida's east coast and in the Bahamas where crews and cargoes were impounded by "the wreckers of New Providence."[62]

The storm struck Charleston at about three o'clock in the afternoon of Friday, October 21, 1797. The like of it "has not been surpassed since that experienced in October, 1783" the local newspaper reported. From the behavior of its winds, expert analysis in recent years has concluded that the storm's eye tracked just to the west of the city.[63] The heaviest winds reportedly started blowing from the southeast, but then shifted to south-southwest. According to the October 21, 1797 edition of the *South Carolina Gazette and Daily Advertiser*, when the storm struck, it did so with

> *such a dreadful degree of violence, accompanied with rain, as to tear away a vast number of vessels from their moorings at the wharves, and did great damage among the shipping and on shore...*
>
> *The violence of the storm continued for about two hours, the wind changing at the latter part of it, to south-southwest with increased violence. The tide was uncommonly high and covered all the wharves.*
>
> *The ship Winyah broke loose from Roper's wharf and, after running foul of several vessels, was driven ashore opposite to Gadsden's wharf.*
>
> *The ships Eliza, O'Neill, Maria, Sheffield, Robinson, sloop Romeo, Tinker and several others were damaged, but not materially, by vessels in drift falling foul of them.*

At the time of this storm, Charleston had a new "aerial chair" or Ferris wheel. It was destroyed. In addition to some ships breaking loose from their moorings, the rigging, sails and hulls of many other vessels were damaged. Smaller boats were driven by the rising water into the surrounding marshes. Roof tiles were blown off and sailed through the air and crashed in the streets, increasing the danger to anyone who, for whatever reason, found themselves outdoors during the tempest. Sadly, a seaman from the brig *Romulus* who found himself outside at Geyer's wharf was washed off a pier and into the turbulent water and drowned.

Other reported storm damage included the collapse of three houses which, unanchored, were blown off their foundations.

As these things go, the storm was mercifully brief or quick moving so the damage was kept to a minimum. "Had the wind continued at southeast it is probable [that] more damage would have been done, but fortunately the southwest wind checked the tide," the *Gazette* reported. Based on water level and damage reports, it appears that this was a category three storm by today's measure.

6.

The Nineteenth Century
Part I

Out of the south cometh the whirlwind.
Job 37:9

The eighteenth century had been relatively kind to South Carolina. Only nine storms had struck. Of those, four (those of 1713, 1722, 1725 and 1752) were very damaging. This relative lull in storm activity would come to an abrupt halt.

October 4, 1800

The first hurricane season of the new century brought with it a harbinger of things to come. Meteorological details of what happened appeared in the Monday, October 6, 1800 edition of the *Charleston Times:*

> *On Saturday night, from eleven to twelve o'clock as tremendous and destructive a storm was experienced in this city and harbor, as has happened for nearly 20 years.*
> *For several days past the wind has been excessively violent from the northeast. On Friday last about noon it shifted to north without any abatement. On Saturday it returned to northeast and blew a very heavy gale until noon accompanied with rain. It then shifted to southeast and continued from that quarter until after twelve o'clock at night, when it suddenly chopped around to southwest and blew with dreadful violence, accompanied with repeated and heavy claps of thunder, and sharp lightening.*

The *Carolina Gazette* of October 9, 1800, provided more detail about what happened to people and property. High tide occurred at nine o'clock on Saturday evening. The wind was blowing from the southeast, causing a great deal of damage to the wharves and the small craft moored at them. More than a dozen small vessels were sunk.

A schooner, commanded by Capt. Wyman, with a valuable cargo of dry goods, bound to Georgetown, was driven against the [ship] New Fleet, mooring on East Bay, and was beat to pieces; her cargo is entirely lost. The New Fleet also met with considerable injury. On South Bay the wharves are much torn up…

At 12 o'clock, or a little after, the gale increased for a few minutes to a species of tornado, and appears to have been most fierce in the northwestern part of the town, and the villages in that quarter, as several houses were blown down and unroofed there. The house of Mr. Christburgh, in Cannonbargh, was amongst the number, and we are sorry to have to add, that Mrs. Christburgh was killed in there by the fall of the house, and [Mr. Christburgh] himself and one of his children severely bruised. A number of chimneys were blown down, as well as trees, and fences, in other parts of the city.

Apprehensions were entertained through the night, and yesterday morning, for the safety of the families at Sullivan's Island; but we are happy in stating that the damage there is very trifling to what might have been expected. The tide was over the greater part of the island, but only three houses were destroyed; those belonging to Col. Morris, Capt. Ormond and Mr. Hunter: their foundations were washed away by the tide. Col. Morris and his family left his house but a few minutes before it fell. We hear of no personal injury having been sustained on the island…

We are sorry to state, that in the gale of Saturday last, a sloop of Capt. Addison's which sailed the day before from Georgetown after having all her sails split to pieces off Cape Roman, drove on shore near Edisto and was entirely beat to pieces. Capt. Rosa, who was her master, and Mr. Thompson, a merchant of Georgetown, were unfortunately drowned. The negroes, sailors, got on shore and were saved.

September 12, 1804

Aaron Burr was on vacation on St. Simon's Island, Georgia, on September 12, 1804, when a hurricane struck. In a letter to his beloved daughter Theodosia of Georgetown County, South Carolina, he described the experience.

In the morning the wind was still higher. It continued to rise, and by noon blew a gale from the north, which together with the swelling of the water became alarming. From twelve to three, several of the outhouses had been destroyed; most of the trees about the house were blown down. The house in which we were shook and rocked so much that Mr. C. began to express his apprehensions for our safety. Before three, part of the piazza was carried away; two or three of the windows burst in. The house was inundated with water, and presently one of the chimneys fell. Mr. C. then commanded a retreat to a storehouse about fifty yards off, and we decamped, men, women and children. You may imagine, in this scene of confusion and dismay, a good many incidents to amuse one if one had dared to be amused in a moment of such anxiety. The house, however, did not blow down.

The storm continued till four, and then very suddenly abated, and in ten minutes it was almost calm. I seized the moment to return home. Before I had got quite over, the gale rose from the southeast and threatened new destruction. It lasted [the] great[er] part of the night, but did not attain the violence of that from the north; yet it contributed to raise still higher of the water, which was the principal instrument of devastation. The flood was about seven feet above the height of an ordinary high tide. This has been sufficient to inundate a great part of the coast; to destroy all the rice; to carry off most of the buildings which were on low lands, and to destroy the lives of many blacks. The roads were rendered impassable, and scarcely a boat has been preserved. Thus all intercourse is suspended.[64]

This storm originated in the West Indies, devastated St. Kitts, sunk many vessels as it crossed the western end of Puerto Rico, passed to the southeast of the Bahamas and took aim at the southeastern coast. It savaged the plantations of the Georgia coast and the city of Savannah. There, one chronicler reported that he had "barely survived the most tremendous hurricane that every blew. The house in which I lodge was blown almost to pieces."[65]

Fort Greene at the entrance to the Savannah River was leveled, "all buildings destroyed, and thirteen lives lost. Muskets were scattered all over the island. Cases of canister shot were carried from one hundred to two hundred feet, and a bar of lead of 300 pounds was likewise removed to a considerable distances. A cannon weighing 4,800 pounds is said to have been carried thirty to forty feet from its position."

Nearby Broughton Island was totally flooded. "[U]pwards of seventy negroes, the property of William Brailsford, were drowned by the oversetting of a boat in which they attempted to escape from the island to the main."

Ironically, a barn in which they may have found shelter on the plantation was spared.

As the storm progressed up the South Carolina coast, its eye struck at Beaufort. The town and surrounding area was left in ruins. All of the dwellings on Bay Point were washed away. Crops were destroyed as a five-foot tidal surge swept across the cotton fields. The causeway that had been built during the previous seven years was washed away in just a few minutes, leaving none of it on the mainland side and only about half on the island side.[66]

The *City Gazette* of September 10, 1804, reported what happened further north in Charleston as follows:

> *On Friday night last, about 11 o'clock, a dreadful gale of wind came on this harbor, and continued to blow with the most extreme violence until Saturday morning, one o'clock; the wind at first was at northeast, in the course of Saturday morning it changed to east, and in the afternoon it changed to southeast. It is impossible for us at this time to describe accurately the destruction caused by this gale; the whole of the wharves from Gadsden's on the Cooper River, to the extent of South-Bay, have received very considerable damage, the heads and sides of most of them are washed away. Of the vessels in the harbor, but three or four have escaped without injury, several are totally lost and many more are much damaged.*
>
> *At seven o'clock on Saturday morning, the period of low water, the tide was as high as it generally is at spring tides: it appeared that at the preceding ebb but little water had left the river; at twelve o'clock it was from two to three feet higher than it had been seen for many years, and made a complete breach over the wharves and drove many vessels on them, where they now lie.*
>
> *On General Gadsden's wharf several stores were washed or blown down, and their contents of rice and cotton much damaged and some lost. On South-Bay, the whole of the bulwark made against the water is in ruins and the house of Mr. William Veitch, built on made ground was washed down. The new street made to continue East-Bay to White Point is greatly damaged, the sea made breaches through it in many places. On Blake's wharf, a brick building occupied as a scale and counting-house, was beat down by the bowsprit of the ship Lydia.*
>
> *In the city no other damage is done than many houses which were covered with slate, are in part unroofed, and most of the trees in the streets and many fences are blown down.*
>
> *Great apprehensions were entertained for the safety of the families on Sullivan's Island, but accounts received from thence yesterday were very*

favorable, not a life was lost there except a black boy. From fifteen to twenty houses were undermined by the water and washed away, the inhabitants of which lost almost everything that was in them.

Eleven ships severely damaged, and five sunk and lost.

As it continued its way up the coast, the storm struck to the west of Georgetown. There the wind first rose out of the northeast at around three o'clock in the afternoon, shifting unto south-southeast around midnight. Crops were destroyed. Buildings were damaged. But there were no reports of lost life in the antebellum town or its surrounding plantations.

The coastal hurricanes of 1806

The year 1806 was a very active storm season. In late August, a violent storm drifted in the Atlantic north of the Bahamas. One ship that put in at Eleuthera reported experiencing a three-day long gale from August 19–21 during its journey. The storm scattered a squadron of French war ships under the command of Jerome Bonaparte, de-masting a number of them. Similarly, the British man-of-war *L'Impeteaux* with seventy-four guns lost its masts and drifted for twenty-three days before being beached.

This storm passed to the east of Charleston, blowing down some trees and forcing some ships ashore, but causing no significant damage. In Georgetown to the north, however, the story was quite different. In a letter to the editor, a plantation owner on the Santee River on the county line about fifty miles north of Charleston and about twenty miles south of the town of Georgetown, wrote:

I never expected to have seen another gale equal to that of September 1804; however, in this neighborhood, we have witnessed a much severer one. On Friday night last it blew, if possible, twice as hard as in the last hurricane— you may imagine how hard when I state there is scarcely a tree left in our yard; such has are not blown up by the roots are broken off, and the roads covered with trees. My rice being planted late has not suffered much, as it was just getting into ear. Had it been three weeks later, I should not have made a barrel. My cotton is completely ruined, twisted and smashed all to pieces, and I do not expect to make ten bales out of 94 acres.[67]

This storm made landfall near Cape Fear in North Carolina. A local newspaper there described it as the "most violent and destructive storm of wind and rain ever known here."[68] That is a powerful assertion coming, as it did, from someone living near the "graveyard of ships"—the point along the coast where the Gulf Stream (which nurtures and drives hurricanes) collides with the cold waters of the Labrador Current flowing from the opposite direction. This hurricane "blew with utmost violence" for over twenty-four hours before abating. "The tide rose to a height hitherto unknown and 'when the wind shifted to southwest it seemed to threaten universal destruction.'"[69]

The storm then drifted away from land. By the time this whirlwind reached the New Jersey coast on Sunday morning, August 24, it was churning the seas most violently. The ship *Rose in Bloom* sunk, taking twenty-one souls to their Creator.

A few weeks later, on September 11 and 12 of 1810, a storm struck Charleston. But because the tide was low and the wind below hurricane force, little damage accompanied it. The *Charleston Courier* of September 14 described what happened this way:

> *A storm of wind and rain has been experienced in this city since Tuesday evening last. The wind, which had been fresh at northeast all day on Tuesday increased toward the evening of that day, and at dark some rain fell; there was but little however in the course of the night.*
>
> *On Wednesday the wind was very high through the day, with an almost incessant fall of rain; the wind increased in the evening to almost complete gale. In the course of the night it hauled around from northeast to southeast and blew with increasing violence; but toward morning it lulled considerably, the rain ceased to fall, and in the course of yesterday, the wind having gotten to the southward and westward, ceased to blow with violence.*
>
> *In the course of Wednesday and Wednesday night some damage was done by the sea to several of the wharves, but we believe that all vessels in port rode out the gale with little or no damage, excepting some small wood sloops, two or three of which sank at the wharves. The street on South Bay, between Meeting and King Streets, was completely washed away by the waves. Several trees were blown down in the streets.*

The "Dreadful Calamity" of 1811

Having dodged two bullets the year before, Charleston's luck ran out (again) in September of 1811. The *Charleston Times* of September 11, under the headlines of *"Dreadful Calamity!!"* reported that

It is our painful duty to detail the awful effects of a dreadful visitation upon our ill-fated city. A tornado having passed through it, carrying death and desolation in its progress.

On Sunday evening, last, the wind, which had been for some days light and variable, shifted to the northeast and blowing very fresh through the night, it continued in the same quarter all day on Monday and Monday Night. On Tuesday morning it blew with increased violence, and during the whole time from Sunday evening, there was almost an unceasing fit of rain. About 10 o'clock in the forenoon on Tuesday, the wind shifted to the southeast and at half past 12 o'clock, a tornado, unprecedented here in its extent and effects, crossed a section of our City. It first took effect at Fort Mechanic, situated on the southeast point of the City, and passed from thence in a northwest direction. It crossed the town in a direct line to the pond of the north side of Cannon's Bridge; how far it has extended its ravages into the country, we have not yet learnt. In its progress, it overturned and completely destroyed a great number of houses and outbuildings, unroofed others, and prostrated trees, fences, brick walls, and almost everything coming in contact with it. It is computed from a hasty view of the scene of devastation that the loss to the City will fall little, if any, short of that experienced by the calamitous fire in October last. But in addition to the great loss of property, we have, on this occasion, to lament the loss of several valuable lives.

The tornado appears to have been about 100 yards in width—after it had penetrated the flag-staff at Fort Mechanic, unroofed the house within the enclosure of that Fort, thrown down the blacksmith's shop contiguous to it, and unroofed all the houses immediately adjoining the Fort, it crossed over to Lynch's Lane, where it unroofed several houses, from thence it proceeded across…to Meeting Street where several houses were unroofed, particularly the large new brick house of Nathanial Russell whose loss in furniture &c…[was] *no less than $20,000.*

From Meeting Street it crossed to Tradd Street where a large three story wooden house on the south side [the property of Mr. J.J. Ehrick] *about half way between Meeting and King Streets was blown down, which damaged two adjoining houses in the fall* [one house being occupied by Mrs. Thomas Harper and the other owned by a Miss Murray, the latter which was damaged beyond repair]. *Most of the houses on the sides of the street, to the corner of King Street, were unroofed or much shattered.*

It [then] *passed up King Street, nearly to Broad Street, unroofing and shattering several houses in its progress, until it reached Broad Street and the house of Dr. Alexander* [last name illegible] *at the northwest corner of Orange Street, and the venerable mansions of the late Dr. [name illegible] on the opposite corner.*

…The most painful part of our duty yet remains—it is to record the deaths which have been occasioned by this dreadful disaster. They are, so far as has come to our knowledge, as follows:

Miss Margaret Collins, aged 21 years killed in a house adjoining Fort Mechanic.

Dr. Conton, a native of France, a worthy man—killed by the falling of his house in Beaufain Street.

Mr. Peterson, a native of Germany, grocer, at the corner of Magazine and Mazyck Streets.

A free Mulatto man, in Church Street-continued.

A French Mulatto girl, in King Street.

Two Mulatto children, either killed or drowned, by the falling of a small wooden house, which was blown into the Mill Pond at Cannon's Bridge.

A Negro man belonging to Dr. Dover, Mazyck Street.

We have also heard of two or three other Negroes killed, but did not learn to whom they belonged.

Besides which, a great number of persons have either had their limbs broken or been very much bruised, and we fear that others have perished whose bodies have not yet been discovered.

Many Charlestonians suffered great financial loss in this storm. Among there were Mr. William Simmons, his wife Affey and their five small children. Their house was blown down and everything inside it was destroyed. They had no money. After spending a brief period of time at the Poor House, the commissioners there had to turn them away.

Homeless and near penniless, Mr. and Mrs. Simmons placed an ad in the September 11, 1811 *Charleston Times*. After describing their circumstances, the ad said that the family

may be found now at the corner of Coming Street, opposite to Bull Street, at Mr. Myme's, to whom they have now resorted for shelter. [They] *feel themselves now compelled to throw themselves on the generosity of a feeling public, for pecuniary assistance. Any and whatever donations may be henceforth bestowed upon them, under the present calamity, will be most gratefully received; and their prayers in return (which is all they now possess) will be unremittingly offered up for the Donors, as somewhat in restitution for the immensity of benefit it will, at the present moment, confer upon them.*

In the evening edition of the paper on September 11, more information about death and destruction was offered. On New East Bay Street, a three-story brick building that housed a blacksmith shop collapsed during the storm. A young lady named Miss Cozzen was killed. Two unnamed blacks, one male and one female, were injured. The adjoining house that was occupied by a Mrs. Warren was "blown to atoms." Three servants in the home of J.H. Stevens on the corner of Water Street and Church Street-continued were injured when the front and part of the north side of the house collapsed. On King Street a double tenement, known by the name of Old Gaul, had the front blown out. Two unidentified mulatto girls and a similarly unnamed white boy were killed there.

The same edition of the paper also sadly reported that a child who had been injured during the storm had died. The newspaper also printed the following "Communication."

In consequence of the late storm, several poor, but worthy families have sustained great damage. It is to be hoped that the citizens of Charleston will come forward, as they have done on so many occasions, and relieve the distressed sufferers; who know not where to go, and are in need of immediate relief. It is hoped that the Intendent and Wardens of the city, whose ears are always open to the distresses of mankind, will open a subscription to all those who are inclined to contribute to the relief of the real sufferers.

The next day, the *Times* provided an extensive addendum to its damage list. Important among the listing was the fact that a two-story house on Magazine Street occupied by Dr. John Conton was leveled to the ground and Dr. Conton killed. On the same street, a two-story house occupied by Misters Archer and Peterson also collapsed, killing Mr. Peterson.

While some twenty people died in the storm, the inconvenience and suffering of the living continued. On Montague Street, the houses of Judge Desaussure and Roger Pinckney were severely damaged, with the north side of the judge's house crushed by a falling chimney. Both houses lost their roofs and, perhaps more importantly, their outhouses. Others suffering losses of their privies were the Duncans, the Roses and the Strobels on Bull Street, and the Carrols on Boundary Street.

All mail service to the north and south was cut by the hurricane. Roads in both directions were impassable. Bridges were washed out by the hurricane that spawned the tornado. So people were left to turn inward, and outward, for inspiration.

Inspiration came two nights later when a comet appeared in the heavens. For two nights it appeared just above the horizon in the north sky in a direct line with the two stars commonly called "the pointers" in the Big Dipper, or Ursa Major, at sunset. The comet remained visible until about eight o'clock each evening. It was described as being as bright as Mars.[70]

On September 17, 1811, the Charleston Times published "A Revised Account of the Tornado!" It estimated the loss of property to be between two and three hundred thousand dollars—a very substantial sum in those days. Regarding the tornado, it noted that "So sudden and unexpected was its approach, that none could foresee it; and so rapid was its progress, and decisive its effects, that none could avoid it."

The phenomena accompanying the tornado, were a continued rain during the preceding day and night, with wind from the north and northeast; and in such a way as to lead to an apprehension of a gale or hurricane, such as we frequently have about this time of year. This wind and rain continued on the forenoon of the day, in rather an increased proportion. For some minutes before it burst forth, there was a complete and dead calm, when it assailed us as before noticed from the southeast. We are not much acquainted with the remote and proximate causes of tornadoes, but we suppose the proximate cause or occasion of this, was a conflicting junction of a current of opposite winds, bearing each a strong and equal impetus, which by clashing produced a new current, nearly we may suppose, at a right angle from their former course. We may also suppose that it either soon diverged, or that its force was soon spent, as we have not heard of much damage done beyond the Ashley River…

There were several instances of very Providential or "hair-breadth scapes"—the most singular was that of two young ladies who were reposing in an upper chamber when a stack of chimneys fell upon the roof, and thence upon the floor of their apartment, precipitating the floor and bed on which they lay, down to the ground floor, being the third story below, and they escaping unhurt. A negro girl, who was in the same room, was killed.

The Thanksgivings that were requested to be offered in the churches for Sunday, for merciful deliverances and escapes, were numerous; and we believe every pulpit represented the present visitation as a warning, to remind us of our duty and our destiny—of the tenure and the issues of life—of the times of danger and the means of safety.

1812—Tragedy on land and sea

U.S. Vice President Aaron Burr's daughter Theodosia was married to South Carolina Governor Joseph Alston. The couple lived on a plantation in Georgetown County. They suffered a profound personal tragedy when their son, Aaron Burr Alston, died in June of 1812. In a letter to his father-in-law, the governor wrote "That boy, on whom all rested; our companion our friend—he who was to have transmitted down the mingled blood of Theodosia and myself—he who was to have redeemed all your glory, and shed new luster upon our families—is dead."[71]

Grief-stricken, Theodosia sought solace in the arms of her kindred. She and her father had always been emotionally very close to one another. Having not seen her father in more than four years, she boarded a ship in Georgetown to sail to New York for a bittersweet reunion. The ship left Winyah Bay and tacked to the northeast, just in time to encounter a furious and powerful storm off Cape Hatteras, North Carolina. Neither she, the ship, its Captain nor crew were ever heard from again. She had joined young Aaron Burr Alston in the hereafter.[72]

After hearing of his daughter's death, Burr wrote his son-in-law "This, then, is the end of all the hopes we had formed...Oh, my friend, if there be such a thing as the sublime of misery, it is for us that it has been reserved."[73]

The storm of August 1813

In addition to the capture and burning of Washington, D.C., the second war between America and Britain involved a great deal of naval maneuvering. American privateers prowled the Carolina coast and elsewhere looking for British shipping to capture. They rationalized their actions as being part of a naval war strategy aimed at stifling British commerce. Many of the ships that were captured were brought to Charleston.

To counter what they regarded as simple piracy, the British positioned the HMS *Mosell* and HMS *Calabri* to blockade Port Royal Sound near Beaufort.

In August 1813, sailors from these ships raided St. Helena and Pinckney Islands, burned a schooner and kidnapped some slaves.

The self-satisfaction of the British did not last long, for within a few days a tropical cyclone struck, forcing the two ships to put to sea, where one of them was lost.[74]

This was the "dreadful storm" of August 27 and 28, 1813. It was one of the most destructive storms to hit post-Columbian South Carolina to its date. As described by one eyewitness writing after the storm from Charleston to a newspaper in Philadelphia[75]

The very foundations of the houses shook. My bedstead had so much motion, that it was not till morn and with incessant fatigue that I got to sleep. In the morning I made a sortie from my lodgings to survey the ravages the storm had made, and the sight was distressing. The trees which afforded a shelter from the scorching rays of the sun were blown down, and lay in every direction in the streets. Slates, tiles, window shutters, signs &c. were scattered over the pavements in quantities.

When I reached the wharves the sight was distressing beyond expression. Every wharf was tore up and at least, one half destroyed. Some were entirely washed away, the logs and timbers washed up into the streets and against the stores; where shallops, boats, shingles, hogsheads, spars, and every individual article that was in or near the wharves was washed promiscuously one over the other, and crushed to pieces.

Every vessel appeared to be more or less damaged, some were thrown partly in the wharves, some sunk in the river, others at the wharves, some were up in the very streets; one large ship was driven against the market and stove part of it in, the smaller vessels were all either up on top of the wharves, or sunk along side.

The guard ship and prison ship drove ashore in James Island, high and dry. I have not heard yet whether any prisoners escaped. Nearly half a mile of Charleston bridge washed away, and drifted on James Island. For want of boats there is no information from Sullivan's Island till the afternoon. I learned that 12 dwelling houses have been blown down and washed away, and 15 to 20 persons drowned. The whole Island was completely inundated four to five feet—the furniture was washed out of many houses. The soldiers from the fort were sent out to afford assistance to some families who were in danger of being washed away. A great many ladies were rescued and taken to the fort, which was the only place of security that was not under water.

Fort Johnson is very much injured; considerable part of it is destroyed. The men's barracks were washed to sea. Many stands of arms, clothing, provisions &c. were also lost. One of the officers told me last evening that they were up to their breasts in water several hours during the night, saving men, women, and children, who were in the barracks, and it was only at the point of the bayonet that they were forced to seek other shelter, although the barracks were then washing away by the sea. To repair the damages and losses sustained at the Fort will require $150,000.

The damage sustained by this city and shipping in rough calculation [was] *estimated at near two million.*

The *Charleston Courier* of August 30, 1813, lamented that

Again we have been visited with one of those disasters which have of late years so frequently desolated our city and seaboard. On Friday night last, we experienced one of the most tremendous gales of wind, that ever was felt upon our coast...

For some days previous to Friday, last, the unsettled state of the weather was such as to indicate a gale; the uncommon roaring of the sea upon the bar, an unerring indication of such an event, was noticed by many...

About 3 o'clock p.m. the wind began to blow very fresh at northeast by east, between 6 and 7 o'clock it had increased to a strong gale, and at 9 o'clock it was a complete hurricane, prostrating in its course houses, chimnies, fences and trees. It continued to blow with equal violence until about one o'clock in the morning when the wind having shifted to the westward, it lulled considerably, but still blew with much force until daylight, when it became moderate.

Torrents of rain accompanied the gale; and the tide, which should have been high before 10 o'clock, continued rising until nearly 12, at which time it was about 18 inches higher than in the great gale of 1804 [when, during that earlier storm, the water was breast deep in some places].

The rising sun, notwithstanding it disclosed to us the ruins produced by the storm, was cheering to the eye; after such an awful night of uncertainty, the return of day was hailed with joy.

The same edition of the *Courier* also reported that

The prison-ship (a large prize brig) at anchor between the town and Castle Pinckney, having on board about 50 prisoners, part of the crew of the Dominica, parted her cables, and was driven by the violence of the gale into the marshes upon James' Island, near Bennett's Mill, where she now lies...

Prioleau's wharf—much injured; the privateer schooner Decatur, with her prize, the Dominica, drove from Lathrop's wharf, across the dock to Prioleau's wharf, where the Decatur brought up with her head and stern on the wharf; both vessels were much injured...

Lathrop's wharf,—the head nearly carried away; all the bridges gone, the ship London Trader, prize to the Decatur, laying at this wharf, broke her fasts and ran foul of the packet ship Belle, stove in the starboard quarter and a part of the stern of the Belle; the London Trader had her larboard quarter stove in, and is otherwise considerably damaged. The Mary Ann's prize Phoenix, which had been repaired at Prichard's wharf was sunk.

Edisto Island to the south of Charleston was exposed to the full brunt of the open sea, but was spared when the wind changed to the north and drove the water back out to sea. Nonetheless, "Those who have long resided here, say that it was the most severe gale which they ever experienced."[76]

While it experienced strong winds and heavy seas that drove two schooners, a sloop and a brig ashore there, Georgetown suffered little physical damage, other than to its wharves.[77] But it did lose about a third of its rice crop and its dirt roads were left "in dreadful condition."[78]

Agricultural losses were compounded between August 29 and September 1, 1815, when a hurricane passed just offshore of the South Carolina coast. Although its eye stayed at sea, wind-driven water flooded rice fields, principally along the Cooper River, damaging much of the crop. Rain also soaked (and ruined) upland cotton fields. This part of the catastrophe for planters was ironic, coming, as it did, at the end of what had otherwise been a long summer's drought.[79]

7.
The Nineteenth Century
Part II

But the wicked are like the tossing sea, which cannot rest, whose waves cast up mire and mud. There is no peace.
Isaiah 57:20–21

The Winyah Hurricane of 1820

Long Bay is an inward curve of shoreline from the North Carolina line to Winyah Bay some sixty miles to the south. The increasingly populated communities of North Myrtle Beach, Atlantic Beach, Myrtle Beach, Surfside Beach, Garden City, North Litchfield and Litchfield Beaches, Pawleys Island, Prince George and Debordieu all lie within the arc of Long Bay. Facing as it does to the southeast and lacking any protection from the open ocean, this entire area is very vulnerable to nature's fury and has repeatedly been struck by hurricanes. The one that hit on September 10, 1820, was described in an edition of the *Winyah Intelligencer* as follows:

> On the 10th instant, we were visited by the most destructive and violent gale of wind which has occurred within the memory of our oldest inhabitants. In this place and in the country, the horrors of it were severely felt, and its effects are visible. Some of our streets [in the town of Georgetown located at the headwaters of Winyah Bay] are rendered almost impassable by the many trees which are lying prostrate, and the mails can neither arrive here, nor depart, so generally have the bridges been washed away.

We have had no direct accounts from the country, but we fear that the crops have suffered. However severely this gale was felt here, it was on the sea-board "fraught with horrors," as the following description of it by a friend will show.

"The gale at North-Inlet was preceded by a great prevalence of easterly and northeasterly winds; but on the 10th the wind blew tempestuously all day, fluctuating between the points east-northeast and northeast; but more generally blowing from the northeast.

"About sunset the scene became truly awful, the wind increasing in violence, and the tide rising with frightful impetuosity. At about this period the Church was blown from its foundation, and many of the inhabitants were seen removing from such houses as appeared most exposed to the dangers of the tide and wind. After dark, the Gale continued to increase, and by 10 or 11 o'clock there raged one of the most violent Hurricanes that has ever been experienced here. At this hour the wind began to 'back' (as it is termed) to the north blowing at times in squalls of incredible violence, bringing with them such floods of rain that there was not a house in the village [that] could entirely resist their fury. The wind about 1 o'clock appeared to have backed as far as the northwest, from which quarter it continued to blow, but with distressing violence, till the morning."

From every investigation which has been made, it appears that the tide rose about 4 feet (perpendicular) higher than the common spring tides, and was as high as the Great Hurricane of 1804. The mercury in the thermometer, as is usual in our Fall Gales, remained during the violence of the storm, without variation—the point at which it stood during this Hurricane was 77½. It began to fall as the Gale subsided, and at 3 o'clock on Monday morning was as low as 72½.

The Church and some other buildings were thrown from their foundations and the house of Mr. John Waldo was completely destroyed. It is with pleasure we add that no lives were lost.

The report went on to say that the stagecoach from Charleston to Georgetown had been delayed by fallen trees and other obstructions in the dirt road, so the passengers exited the coach, mounted the horses and rode on. "Dr. A. Solomon was riding on, when a tree falling, and only on the horse's withers, crushed the horse to death. The Doctor happily found himself uninjured."

Almost all the crops in Georgetown—by then one of South Carolina's most productive rice producing areas—were destroyed.

In his comprehensive study of Atlantic coastal hurricanes for the American Meteorological Society in 1963, David M. Ludlum postulated that from all available evidence it appeared that the center of this storm passed inland north of the town of Georgetown. Reports from Charleston described "a smart gale from the north-northeast" had been accompanied by heavy rain. It had started around midnight on September 10 and was blowing from the west by dawn. The damage was limited to trees around Charleston being stripped of leaves, fruit and small branches.

From North Carolina reports, David Ludlum computed that the storm made landfall somewhere in Long Bay (to the south of Cape Fear) and then curved out to the northeast past Ocracoke and Cape Hatteras. This tracking was supported by information that "A ship off Ocracoke Bar met a heavy southeast gale on the 10th and then experienced an almost dead calm at 0630 on the 11th when a waterspout passed over the ship. Another gale commenced in the afternoon."[80]

This, obviously, was the eye of the storm. And while it was certainly a severe storm, an even more serious one followed just two years later.

The troubles of 1822

In early 1822, Denmark Vesey, Peter Poyas, William Garner, Ned Bennett and Gullah Jack finalized a plan for a slave uprising to begin at midnight on July 4, 1822. Some six thousand slaves were to be recruited to seize the city of Charleston, burn it down, kill the white men, seize the ships in the harbor and sail for Santo Domingo.

On May 30, 1822, Vesey and the others were betrayed by a house servant who told authorities that she had been asked to join the revolt. The man who tried to recruit her, William Paul, was arrested and ultimately confessed after being interrogated. Paul implicated Peter Poyas and another man named Mingo Harth.

Hearing of these events, Vesey changed the date of the uprising from July 4 to June 16. Two days before the scheduled uprising, a second house servant confessed involvement. Five military companies were activated. Vesey and many others were arrested. He and thirty-five others were tried and hanged. Another thirty-two were transported from the Americas to a slow death at hard labor in the tropics.

Whites were panicked, fearful that their decades of cruelty had produced unwanted retribution. As they scrambled to maintain their position of dominance, disaster called in another form.

On Friday evening, September 27, 1822, an "equinoetial gale"[81] struck the South Carolina coast. Around ten o'clock that evening the wind began to blow out of the northeast across Charleston. It shifted around midnight to the north when it "assumed the desolating power of a West Indian Hurricane."[82] Shortly after, the wind shifted again, this time to the northwest where it continued to increase in velocity. Its fury was sustained until about 2:30 a.m. in the pre-dawn hours of September 28 "when it suddenly ceased and dropped into 'grim repose.'"[83] The fury of the storm was gone by three o'clock in the morning. But during the relatively short time that it had unleashed its fury on Charleston,

> *the petty works of man were prostrated and shattered to pieces by the breath of Heaven. Trees, barns, stables, roofs, fences &c. all that stood before this irresistible agent, were carried away. Some houses have had their roofs shattered and precipitated on their owners' heads. Others have been overthrown—chimnies toppling—the doors and windows of others carried away by the blast, and everything of light ornament or delicate structure torn off and their foundations shaken. The voice of the tempest was equally awful. It resembled the shrieks of a Damon of the air, while its invisible and mighty hands were scattering destruction.*
>
> *The cover to the cupola of the Circular Church in Meeting Street (of sheet tin) was lifted and carried several hundred yards, and fell in Queen Street. It is about sixty feet in circumference and resembles the shield of the Titans.*
>
> *The loss sustained by land and by water, we are not at present able to estimate…But the destruction of property is of no consideration, when we think of the loss of lives. Mr. Laval, whose residence was at Hampstead, has been severely wounded by the oversetting of his house, and his wife and two children killed! Two negroes of Mr. Laval's were also killed, and Mr. John Wilson, butcher, who was on a visit but detained by the storm, was buried under the ruins. Several dead bodies have been picked up in the river, four of them negroes of Captain Saltus and a white man…*
>
> *From Sullivan's Island, our accounts are of the most shocking nature. We understand that upwards of fifteen houses have been blown down, and others more or less injured. The residence of Mr. Lewis Morris Jr. was overset by the tempest—his wife and eldest son together with Mr. Austece, private tutor, were all three killed. Mr. Morris's house was considered one of the safest on the Island. How vain is human security!*
>
> *The hour of fancied safety is frequently the moment of destruction. Mrs. Middleton, wife of Mr. Thomas Middleton, in attempting to rush from her residence, which she thought was falling to pieces, was*

accompanied by her husband, from whose protecting arms the tempest snatched her, and in her distraction she wandered away and was afterwards found drowned on the beach...

In the fall of Mr. Lewis Morris's house (mentioned above) a negro man was killed and a negro woman had her thigh broke.

...Colonel Johnson's house [was] blown down, and a mulatto child killed...

Mr. Boyce and family had a most providential escape—they had just left the shed room in which they slept, for a place of greater safety, when the whole of it fell...

Captain Clark with two negroes of the packet boat Eagle [were] drowned...A negro fellow who clung to the keel of the boat stated that Captain Clark, finding it impossible to come into the wharf with security [tried to] swing around to South Bay. He has not since been seen...

A negro girl, belonging to Mr. R. Adger, was killed by the falling of the roof of a house on King Street...

In all, there have been about thirty-five deaths.

Among the public buildings that were damaged in Charleston during the storm, were "the beautiful City Hall," the jail, the workhouse, the theatre and nearly every house of worship.

As described in the *Charleston Courier* on September 30, "The havoc occasioned by this tremendous visitation in the city is without parallel in the memory of our oldest inhabitants. The Tornado, which passed over a part of it, in the year 1811, was perhaps equal or even greater violence, but its effects were then confined to a very narrow limit, while the desolation of this occasion is extended to every part of the city and suburbs."

In the belief that the sun's passage across the equator at the autumn equinox caused big storms, the reporter for the *Charleston Gazette* opined that

The unfortunate confidence which several families continued on the Island until the Equinoctial sometimes arises from the intermission, only for one season, of these rude and dangerous visitors. The safest plan would be not to trust to chance—which proves so often fatal—although we sometimes escape it. Let us not raise a rule of action out of a few exceptions. On the contrary, let us be taught by the sad lessons we almost annually receive. Those who will not show (to use the vigorous language of Johnson) "that hope can triumph over experience."[84]

While his science may have been wrong, the reporter's advice was sound.

David Ludlum in *Early American Hurricanes*[85] identified the point of landfall for this storm as being about halfway between the ports of Charleston and Georgetown. Ludlum tracked the storm on a course slightly to the west of due north as it continued inland. That track put Georgetown on the very deadly left hand side of the storm.

The Georgetown newspaper of the day, the *Winyah Intelligencer*, in its October 5, 1822 edition, described what happened there as follows:

The weather had been for a week or ten days very unpleasant, the wind blowing occasionally fresh from the east and southeast, but as there appeared none of those indications which usually precede a hurricane, and as the mercury in the thermometer continued low, very little apprehension was entertained; even at sunset Friday evening the 27th instant although the weather was bad, yet there appeared no cause to apprehend a gale.

At the close of the day there was a heavy shower from the southeast accompanied by some wind, after which the weather appeared better. Between ten and eleven o'clock, however, we had a squall from the northeast from which quarter the wind continued to blow high till about 12, when we experienced another more violent squall from about east.

The mercury about this hour had risen from 79, and continued to rise for some time after. From 12, the wind continued gradually to change from southeast and south, increasing in violence as it shifted; from southeast it blew with frightful and unprecedented violence. Most of the injury caused by the wind must have occurred about 2 o'clock in the morning...

At the time of high water...about seven o'clock in the evening, the inhabitants apprehended no danger from the tide, as, from the violence of the gale, it was presumed that it could not continue until the period of the succeeding high water. In this expectation, however, it pleased the Almighty to disappoint them, and by the awful result, to prove how fallacious are all human calculations.

The tide could have ebbed little at all, when the waters returned with irresistible violence, and between 3 and 4 o'clock in the morning had reached a height far exceeding that of the gale of 1804, and we believe of any other tide within the memory of the oldest inhabitants—a very small portion of [North] Island remained above the ocean.

The gale began to subside, we believe, about half past 3 o'clock, the wind then blowing from southwest. It was oppressively warm during the gale, and many of those luminous bodies, or meteors, unusual in fall gales, passed near the surface of the earth. The gale was of shorter duration and accompanied by less rain than usual.

As the newspaper reported, North Island at the mouth of Winyah Bay was completely under water. More than 120 slaves and 5 of their self-appointed masters were drowned on North Island. Throughout the area, the total loss of life in the storm has been estimated at around 300.

James McDowel, a Scotchman by birth and rice planter, was staying at his summerhouse on North Island when the storm hit. "That night, his house was washed away, and to his horror, he saw his wife and children for the last time, struggling in the surging billows of the waters of North Inlet, now mingled in one body with the mighty Atlantic Ocean, while he escaped death by being dashed upon the bank of the mainland."[86]

Eight miles inland, at the county seat of Georgetown County, the *Winyah Intelligencer* reported,

The Court-House…sustained very serious injury, and many of the records of the Clerk's Office [were] destroyed. The Sheriff's Office had every door and window blown in and the records and papers destroyed. The four chimnies of the Jail [were] blown down and the building in other respects much injured. Many of the tiles [were] blown from the roof of the Bank. The building over the Market, occupied by the Town Council, is nearly down, every pillar which supports it being fractured.

At nearby Debordieu Beach, the house of Dr. Levy Myers was carried out to sea in the storm with the doctor and fifteen members of his family inside. They were never seen nor heard from again.

Twenty-plus miles inland, in adjoining Williamsburg County, the storm "came from an eastern direction, continuing a few hours and then there was a calm, but before the people could kindle up a fire, it returned from the west with greater violence and destruction." Little children "huddled together on and around their parents' knees in one corner of a big room sheltered and covered with blankets, quilts, etc. to keep out the drenching rain and boisterous wind; the next morning the little white and colored children played…in the gable end of the house which had been blown off."[87]

Saul Parsons was on his way home from the town of Kingstree when the storm struck. He was on horseback, riding down the narrow dirt lane through the pinewoods. He took refuge at "the McCrea old place" under a large, ancient oak tree.

Parsons and his horse sheltered themselves as best they could from the wind and rain. Then, suddenly, it became calm. Thinking the storm over, Parsons mounted his steed and started home. He had not gone far when the backside of the eye wall struck. He rode hurriedly back to the oak tree, only to find that it had been uprooted and blown over.

> *Nothing more is known for the next two miles, as to how or in what manner Mr. Parsons made the trip, but to picture his situation amid thousands of falling trees, in the howling tempest of wind and rain to an unprecedented extent.* [Then], *at the very first opportunity to open a door and look out on the waste and destruction everywhere expected, old Mr. Alexander McCrea found Mr. Parsons safe and sound crouched up under a bench on his piazza, and his horse standing at the door steps.*

Parsons and his horse "had defied the storms, tho' they did their level best or mightiest on [this] man and his horse."[88]

Again, crops were in ruins, this time in a wide swath across Charleston, Georgetown, Williamsburg, Florence and the other counties in the storm's path.

Many of the people of the South Carolina Lowcountry and Pee Dee region spent the next weeks "gathering up corn on the ground in the fields, cutting trees off the fences and righting them…clearing the roads" and the like. The amount of work to be done was staggering. Just as one small example, in one two-mile stretch of road near Indiantown Presbyterian Church in Williamsburg County, some four hundred trees were reported to have been blocking the road.[89]

After leaving death and destruction in its path, the storm continued across North Carolina and into Virginia. At his estate in Virginia, Thomas Jefferson's granddaughter experienced the storm, describing it in a letter as "a violent storm which strewed the whole mountain top with broken boughs of trees, and tore one of our willows completely asunder."[90]

The storm also dumped torrential rains on the Blue Ridge Mountains in western Virginia. While the storm lasted only about twelve hours there, enough rain fell to swell the Staunton River to "the greatest height ever known," sweeping away crops that only a few days before were wilting in a prolonged drought.[91]

Back on North Island, among many other chores, surviving slaves were put to task building storm towers or turrets in which to seek refuge in future storms. As it turned out, those would save many of their descendents' lives in another killer storm near the end of the century.[92]

One enduring legend from this particular storm is that of the Gray Man of Pawleys Island. This apparition has wandered the beaches there ever since 1822, warning residents and visitors of impending storms. The spirit is said to be that of a young man who had been touring Europe for several years. He had just arrived home. After paying his respects to his family on Pawleys Island, he rode south with a slave along the beach. He was riding to North Inlet a few miles away to meet with his fiancé. He had not seen her in several years.

Happy to be home and feeling playful, he challenged his servant to a race. The two men urged their horses on. Hoping to gain an advantage, the young man took a shortcut over a dune and through the marshes at Middleton Pond. As he raced along, the young suitor's horse stumbled. The man fell off and into quicksand. In a short time, both he and his horse were sinking deeper and deeper. The servant's efforts at rescue were unavailing. The young man and his horse sunk below the surface.

On hearing the news of her lover's death, the young girl was grief-stricken. She wandered the beaches of North Inlet, Debordieu and Pawleys Island seeking solace in nature's beauty. Then, one afternoon as she was walking along the beach, the wind came up from the northeast. In the ocean spray in front of her she saw a man looking out at the sea. He was dressed in gray. He warned her to stay away, but she could not. There, in the mist, was her lost lover. He told her that she and her family must leave the island immediately.

Distraught, the young girl ran home and told her father what she had seen. He thought she had gone crazy, so he arranged to take her to a famous doctor in Charleston. The entire family made the trip. Shortly after they left, the hurricane of 1822 struck, sweeping homes out to sea with their occupants still inside.

Ever since 1822, the Gray Man has been seen before major storms have struck Pawleys Island and is said to be the island's most reliable weather forecaster.[93]

The flood of 1824

While escaping a direct hit (the hurricane struck somewhere between Savannah, Georgia, and Jacksonville, Florida), antebellum residents of South Carolina learned first-hand about the secondary effects of tropical cyclones in the middle of September of 1824.

As this storm traveled inland, it dumped tremendous quantities of rain in the Piedmont. In Sumter County near the middle of the state, 9.2 inches of water fell during the storm. Mature crops ready for harvesting were destroyed. On the plantation of famous South Carolinian Wade Hampton, crop damage exceeded $35,000.[94] His was only one of hundreds of farms and plantations in the midlands of the state. That water then flowed downhill and downstream, flooding fields throughout the Lowcountry. Agricultural losses were in the millions when all the damage across the state was computed.

The early June storm of 1825

The nation's economy had fallen into serious depression after the Panic of 1819.[95] Still suffering under the weight of that economic calamity, those dependent on agriculture in South Carolina's Lowcountry and adjoining areas (meaning just about everyone) were dealt repeated blows by serious crop damage in hurricanes of 1820 and 1822 and the floods of 1824. But more misery was to come.

In early June of 1825, a serious storm was reported brewing off Florida's eastern coast. A fast-moving weather system, it reached full hurricane force by the time it reached Charleston on Friday morning, June 3. The storm blew for most of the day, ripping up trees, throwing down fences and causing general havoc in the city.[96] From this description it appears that the storm had reached category one stage by the time it reached Charleston.

As it progressed up the coast through northern Charleston County and through Georgetown and Horry counties the hurricane strengthened. As it did, it flooded fields, caused heavy crop losses, drowned livestock, uprooted trees and knocked down fences and small outbuildings. The sloop *Leopard* out of Bridgeport, Connecticut, came across an abandoned ship adrift with her main mast and rudder gone. The name on the back of the vessel was the *Argo of New York*. No one was on board, but there were open trunks on the deck with clothing scattered about. Her log was found. It indicated that she had sailed from New Orleans twelve days earlier.

Waterlogged, the ship was towed to Beaufort, North Carolina, but because it was so low in the water it ran aground on the bar near the entrance to the port. Only its cargo was salvaged: 350 barrels of pork, 400 bales of cotton and 90 bundles of tobacco.[97]

Eleven sailing vessels sought shelter at Elizabeth City, North Carolina, to ride out the storm. None escaped undamaged. Two were sunk and the rest ran aground. At Ocracoke, sixteen ships sunk. Three more were driven out to sea by the current and lost at sea with their crews still aboard. The schooner *Eliza & Mary*, laden with coffee, was cast ashore.[98]

Damage throughout the area was summarized as "incalculable…most of the valuable timber and forest trees are blown down, many houses blown down, horses killed and much stock destroyed."[99]

The storm's path of destruction continued through Virginia, along the New Jersey coast, past New York City, along the coast of Long Island and past Nantucket and Cape Cod before spinning away into the north Atlantic. As it made its journey, winds spinning off it knocked down trees in front of Independence Hall in Philadelphia. Every community it passed suffered. Many sailors died. The Colombian frigate *Venezuela* was driven ashore. The schooner *Hornet* sank, taking her crew to a watery grave. "We never recollect a storm in June of equal severity or duration. It was more like a regular and furious equinoctial than anything else; and being unlooked for, has, no doubt, been more extensively calamitous."[100]

More fearful events were yet to come.

Troubles in Georgetown

In 1827, an offshore hurricane made its way along the South Carolina coast on August 23 and 24. It was first reported in the Windward Islands on August 17, at St. Martin's and St. Thomas August 18, passing Haiti August 19, the Turks on August 20 and the Bahamas on August 20 and 21. It ultimately made its landfall somewhere between Cape Fear and Cape Hatteras. But while off the South Carolina coast, its winds blew here "with great violence." It having passed on low tide, it caused little physical damage.[101] But it may have served as a harbinger of an ill wind that was soon to blow across Georgetown.

On July 23, 1829, Captain William Vaught of the Lower All Saints Beat Company (a legislatively mandated runaway slave patrol) learned about a slave uprising that was being planned in Georgetown County. Outnumbered eight or nine to one by their slaves, Georgetown's privileged planters were extremely alarmed. Fifteen slaves were arrested. Their leaders were named Quacooo, Mood and Charles Prioleau. Quacooo and Mood were the "property" of Francis Kinloch, the owner of Kensington, WeeHaw and Rice Hope plantations. Prioleau was a slave to John Coachmen.

All three men were tried and convicted. Charles Prioleau was hanged along with another unnamed co-conspirator. Quacooo and Mood were "transported" to the tropics. Each participant who testified favorably was returned to his "master's protection, kindness, [receiving] every necessary support for his sustenance and comfort."[102]

These events were followed one year later by a very destructive hurricane. The storm first started brewing in the vicinity of the Leeward Islands and turned into a full force hurricane near the Virgin Islands on August 12 and 13. It passed between the Bahamas and the Florida coast on August 14 and 15, the Georgia coast on August 16 and then along the South Carolina coast.[103]

The storm passed a short distance seaward of Charleston and caused no damage there that was reported in the press. Further up the coast, however, the story was somewhat different.

As the storm blew and dumped heavy rains, the earthen impoundments around the rice fields in Georgetown County—and, in particular, those along the northern shore of Winyah Bay—began to give way. That left a great deal of the rice crop unprotected from the brackish water that was being driven by wind and tide. As the water rose, the banks of fields on the southern side of the bay began to collapse too. More than half of the rice crop was lost.[104] Some planters were left with little more rice than was necessary to plant the next year's crop.[105] The *Winyah Intelligencer* described the storm as "the most severe gale since that of 1822" when 120 slaves and 5 others drowned on North Island at the mouth of Winyah Bay. Fortunately, this time there was shelter from the storm. The turrets the slaves had built two years earlier protected them from the high water, if not from fear, this time.

The "unequaled gale" of 1834

Beaufort, Charleston and the environs in between experienced a good bit of rain and modest damage on Thursday, September 4, 1834 as strong northwest winds from a storm that remained off the coast passed through the area. "The wind being from a quarter favorable to the safety of shipping, we understand that they sustained no damage—but in the city, a great number of trees were upturned and broken off; some of the slates on the houses broken off, and in several instances the roofs injured; and many fences in the outskirts of the city were prostrated,"[106] is how one newspaper reported events in the lower coast.

The same newspaper informed its readers that there was no wind or rain at Aiken or forty miles inland on the railroad line to Columbia.

The description of modest damage in Charleston and the absence of damage a short distance inland indicate that the storm stayed offshore as it passed the southern South Carolina coast.

In Georgetown to the north, the story was quite different. The storm carried with it a tremendous flood tide. Rice fields were submerged by salt water for nearly twelve hours. According to "one of our respectable and oldest citizens," the tide was higher than in the 1804 hurricane. "The fatal storm of 1822 was of short duration; and by a sudden change in the wind the water was driven back and did not rise near as high as in 1804" the September 4 edition of the *Georgetown Union* reported. While the 1822 storm had destroyed homes, a church and took many lives on North Island, the paper opined that this storm of 1834 was more furious, of longer duration and much more destructive of property. For as "far as the eye could reach, the fields were covered, and but for the appearance here and there of a tree or cluster of bulrushes, vines &c. we should not have known that valuable plantations lay under the overwhelming waters. It seemed much as if Old Chaos was about to come again," the *Georgetown Union* reported. To help illustrate just how severe the flooding was, news accounts from North Carolina put the water in the Cape Fear River at forty-six feet above flood stage.[107] Crop, timber, livestock and game losses were severe.

A destructive decade

To compound the misery experienced in the preceding year, the following year a very severe storm made landfall south of Savannah. While it moved inland of Charleston (where little harm was caused), strong winds and heavy rains from it caused a very high storm tide to surge into Winyah Bay in Georgetown County to the north. The water reached a height of just two feet below that of the hurricane of the previous year. "The usual crop destruction reports came in from the plantations," is the matter of fact way the *Georgetown Union* reported the situation on September 21, 1835. But, once again, the local economy was sent reeling.

Two years later in 1837, a very active hurricane season brought "Racer's Hurricane" ashore at the Alabama/Florida Gulf Coast boundary. The storm then followed a track across central Georgia and through the midlands and Pee Dee section of South Carolina before entering the Atlantic at the southeastern North Carolina coast. It caused a great deal of flooding, destroyed valuable timber and severely damaged crops in its path.

An immense, destructive storm, it got its name from the first ship to encounter (and survive) a three-day ride in it through the lower Caribbean, H.M.S. *Racer*. During the time it was over water, this hurricane wrecked the brigs *Perseverance, Jane, Elbe, Phoenix*, the schooners *Select, Henry, Star, Lady of the Lake, Helen* and *Correo*, along with the privateer *Tom Toby*, the Texan naval schooner *Brutus* and the steamboats *Merchant, Columbia, Pontchartrain* and *Mobile* in the Gulf of Mexico.

Along the Gulf coast "[m]en, women and children were seen floating upon boards, logs and small boats, for days and nights…homeless residents were seen wandering about in despair, gathering something from the wreck to hide their nakedness, or to save them from starvation.[108]

After entering the Atlantic Ocean the same storm struck the newly constructed steamboat *Home* on its way from New York City to Charleston. As the ship floundered in the turbulent seas off Cape Hatteras, she began to leak. The leaking became so bad that the captain required all hands aboard, passengers included, to bail. The strategy did not work. The engine room flooded and the ship grounded just south of the Cape. Of the 130 souls on board, only 40 made it safely through the roaring surf to shore.[109]

The loss of the *Home* was the second tragedy for a Charleston-based ship during this hurricane season. In early August, the Packet S.S. *Mills* sunk in the third storm of the season off Jekyll Island, taking fourteen of the fifteen persons on board with it. The ship was on its way from Charleston to St. Augustine when it ran into heavy seas.

Two years later, in late August of 1839, another storm roared up the South Carolina coast. The gale began around 5:00 p.m. on the evening of August 28 in Charleston with winds out of the northeast. They shifted to the northwest at 6:00 a.m. on August 29. The wind finally ceased around 1:30 p.m. But because the storm was far enough out at sea, no damage resulted anywhere in South Carolina—none, that is, except the fear and foreboding of the now storm weary and traumatized residents.

12. Not even the might oak can withstand a hurricane's fury.

13. Colonial beach house on Pawleys Island damaged by Hugo.

14. Guardsmen take a much-needed break during post-storm patrol.

15. Not the best way to catch a crab.

16. Pawleys Island suffers another loss in the storm.

17. More damage at Pawleys Island.

18. Antebellum cottage succumbs to Hugo.

19. After the water receded.

20. Lifeline.

21. This house cannot be salvaged.

22. Huge sand dunes washed away by Hugo.

23. Not the outer limits of destruction.

24. Turn-of-the-century Georgetown recovering from the 1893 storm. *Courtesy of Morgan Collection, Georgetown Public Library.*

25. Graveyard. *Courtesy of NOAA.*

26. Rice fields in Georgetown destroyed in the 1893 storm. *Original painting at City Hall, Georgetown.*

27. Waterspouts. *Courtesy NOAA.*

28. The Ben Sawyer Bridge after Hugo. *Courtesy NOAA.*

29. Used boats for sale. *Courtesy NOAA.*

8.
The Nineteenth Century Part III

If he holds back the waters, there is drought; if he lets them loose, they devastate the land.
Job 12:15

The violent storm of 1854

Thankfully, there was a lull in hurricane activity in South Carolina for the next baker's dozen of years between 1840 and 1853. While the state felt the effects of a storm that passed inland from the Florida Gulf in August of 1851 (with moderate crop damage) and August of 1852 that originally made landfall in Louisiana (heavy rain, but no reported damage in South Carolina),[110] the humanity of the state, black and white, had a chance to catch its collective breath and allow fear of nature's fury to ebb.

Then on what was the fiftieth anniversary of the great gale of 1804 that killed five hundred people between Georgia and North Carolina on September 7, 8 and 9, tragedy struck once again. On the morning of September 7, 1854, a gale began to blow from St. Simon's Island, Georgia to Charleston. The newspapers of the day tell the story of what happened in South Carolina most adequately.

The *Courier* of Charleston on September 8, 1854, read:

> *Early yesterday morning, a heavy northeast gale visited our city, which continues unabated at the present moment—2 A.M. At noon the rain*

commenced to fall with considerable violence, but ceased in about an hour, although at intervals throughout the day and night there were several showers. So far, however, we have heard of no injuries sustained by the shipping, and a hasty visit just paid to the wharves, satisfies us that all the vessels are well secured. Several left their berths at an early period in the day, and sought shelter either in Ashley river, or at its mouth; but if the wind does not shift round from its present quarter, we have no fear that any serious damage will be sustained; and even should it do so; the precautions adopted by the various commanders will mitigate considerably the apprehensions that otherwise would be entertained.

By the following morning, September 9, 1854, the storm had gained strength. The *Courier* updated its readers thus:

We are called upon to record one of the severest and most destructive storms that have been felt at our port for many years. In duration, violence, and amount of damage, we can, indeed, compare the visitation which has just passed over with nothing that has occurred since the memorable gale of 1804—of which, by a strange coincidence, the present was the semi-centennial anniversary.

The first indication and warning appeared at a very early hour of Thursday morning, or soon after the midnight of Wednesday. The breeze was from the Northeast and gradually increasing amounted to a gale about midnight on Wednesday. From this period it continued with occasional…and with violent aggressions, throughout the whole of yesterday. The direction was changed frequently, and there were brief intervals of comparative quiet, and as like been usual in our severe gales, the wind, for the greater portion of its violent duration, settled down at, or nearly, in the Southeast.

The violence of the storm, which was accompanied mostly by heavy drifts and falls of rain, together with the excitement and confusion necessarily attending such an occasion, prevented us from obtaining such a statement of particulars as would justify even an approximate estimate of damages. We have seen and heard enough, however, to force the conviction that the aggregate of loss in or near the city itself will be heavy, and it will be swelled fearfully, we apprehend, by the reports we shall in due time receive, of the damages at a distance, and along our coast and rivers. We can but specify now, such items of damages as we have been able to ascertain.

All the wharves along on East Bay have suffered more or less. Some have been severely damaged, the planking and posts being carried away, while a number have also been injured in their head walls. The water overflowed them completely and flooded the warerooms, store houses and counting offices.

In addition to the wharf property injured, there has been in this way a serious loss sustained in the total or partial destruction of merchandise in store. On Brown's wharf alone the destruction of two thousand sacks of salt is reported, with serious damage done in sugar, of which there was also a considerable stock...The loss of the wharves generally, is roughly estimated now at $250,000 to $300,000.

The City in its corporate capacity has suffered a heavy loss in the damage to the Battery. The woodwork, with a large portion of the stone in the facing of both sides East and South, has been destroyed. The water formed breaches at the swells of the flood even over the highest points, and the spray was dashed in considerable quantities on the roofs of houses opposite, on the West side. The bridge causeway leading to the Bathing House off the point, has been carried away, and the House itself considerably damaged. The wharves along South Bay have all been seriously injured—Moreland's wharf having been cut away nearly to the low water mark.

The causeway at the west end of Tradd Street, which was built a few years ago, at a heavy cost, by the city and Mr. Chisolm, has been utterly destroyed.

Mills' Mud Machine has been sunk at its place off the wharf, and will be lost it is supposed.

There was not a very large amount of shipping in harbor, and from the careful preparations made in advance, the damages thus sustained have been less than was at first apprehended from the severity of the gale. We briefly state the particulars:

At Union wharf, the barks St. Lawrence and Aquatic carried away the wharf posts—the latter being much chafed, while the former escaped injury.

At Central wharf, the schooner Lucy Wetham parted her bow fasts, and was borne over against the schooner J. N. Muir—both receiving considerable damage by the shock.

At Atlantic wharf, the steamer DeKalb had her cabin roof blown off, with other slight injuries. The brig Adela carried off the wharf posts with her bow lines, but escaped injury. The schooner Isabella,

Capt. Gage, at North Atlantic wharf, sank, we regret to learn, at about nine o'clock last evening.

At Southern wharf, the brig Eureka, which was discharging [cargo], *broke her moorings and drifted against and along the Battery, striking heavily on the stone work. She was thrown also against the Bathing House, which was damaged as above stated, and finally driven around into Ashley river, and is now a complete wreck near the mouth of Wappoo cut.*

Several schooners and smaller craft have been driven on shore in the marsh, near Laurens Street…

The ship Lydia, at Vanderhorst's wharf, parted her fasts and drifted against Adger's wharves, but without serious injury up to a late hour of the day. The schooners Parker and Charleston, both from Georgetown, with shingles, have been sunk—the former at Commercial wharf, and the latter off the Mount Pleasant Ferry wharf…

In the southern and southwestern portions of the city there was an extensive area over flooded to the depth of several feet. The space south of Broad Street, and west of Logan Street, including the greater portion of Franklin and South Streets, was an uninterrupted lake.

Many yards and gardens to the southeast were also flooded, and the occupants of several houses were compelled to retreat in boats. The out-buildings of Mr. Jose Dawson, at the water end of Limehouse Street, where undermined and carried off, and the foundations of his dwelling house seriously impaired. The water reached up Calhoun Street from the east to Meeting Street, and we learn also that the flood reached the line of the South Carolina Rail Road, near Payne's farm.

The average height, as compared with previous great floods, we cannot state, but in many portions it reached to marks and points considered beyond even the probable limits of such floods.

At Castle Pinckney the sentry house and a portion of the bridge attached, were torn loose and drifted against Brown's wharves.

The anxiety to hear from Sullivan's Island during the greatest violence of the storm was painfully distressing. Throughout the day communication was totally interrupted, as no vessel could have effected a landing at the time. The wharf and house of the Mt. Pleasant Ferry Company at the foot of Market Street have been swept away; and there is no doubt that the destruction of property at the Island itself has been considerable. In the afternoon the steamer Aid, Capt. Payne, left the city for the purpose of communication with the

Island, but found it impossible, and was forced to seek safe mooring in Ashley River.

At about ten o'clock last night a party of seven, at the risk of their lives, reached the city from the Island, which they lad left in a good boat at about four in the afternoon, but we could glean but little information from the member of it whom we saw—in fact, as he stated all were so absorbed in saving their effects that little attention was paid to what was transpiring elsewhere. McNulty's house was swept away at an early period of the storm, but whether life was lost thereby our informant could not say.

At the Moultrie House, the sea…[was] making a clear breach though the ground floor. Those in it had taken refuge in the cupola. The majority, however, of the inmates were safely lodged in Fort Moultrie, where, we presume, all who considered themselves in danger had also gone…The Island was perfectly deluged, but, as far was we could learn, no reports were current of any loss of life.

The instances of damage by the gale are numerous but, we trust, will not be found to reach a very large amount. The tiling and slating of many houses have been injured, and tin roofing has been blown off entirely in some cases. This was done, with the large block store on Meeting Street, from Hayne to Market, occupied on the first floor by Townsend, Crane & Co. The injuries threatened, in consequence by leakage, were such that a considerable portion of the stock had to be removed into neighboring stores, and some damage has been sustained. A large portion of tin roofing on the Charleston Hotel was also borne off, and much damage was done to the new dome in the area of that establishment. A two story wooden building, with brick foundations, in King near John Street, and belonging, we believe, to Mr. C. Dunn, was blown down.

The storm, if prevailing over any extent to the degree which marked it here, will involve an immense loss, and even in the immediate vicinity, the damages sustained by planters must be most serious. The staple crops, whose promising inspect and encouraging auguries we noticed but a week since, were in a stage that rendered them peculiarly liable, and we have good reason to apprehend the hopes previously indulged, on good grounds by very many of our planters, have been almost utterly blasted…

The previous gales recorded as the most violent and destructive, occurred in 1752 and 1783. The subsequent gales that were especially memorable, were in 1811 and 1822.

Given the serious storms that had afflicted other parts of South Carolina during the first half of the nineteenth century, this last comment represented Charleston chauvinism in its purest form.

Under the headline "The Late Gale—Its Effects," the evening edition of the paper ran the following story:

> *Our city on Saturday presented a mournful aspect in many portions, and bore striking evidences of the violence and destructive energies of the great gale and flood tide of Friday morning.*
>
> *The damages in some points were even beyond our first anticipation—and it will be [a] long [time] before the traces of destruction and havoc can be removed even from the city itself.*
>
> *Among the prominent buildings that have been severely damaged by the wind and rain, we must place the Charleston Hotel, which has sustained very heavy damages. The wing on Pinckney Street, and the back or east wing, forming together one half of the quadrangle of the building, were unroofed at an early period in the storm on Friday, and the tin roofing was blown in large masses against the chimnies, causing the fall of four of them on the dome of the new and elegant saloon which had recently been erected in the central area through the enterprise of Mr. Kixer, who had also repaired and improved and refurnished the house in other respects. The falling of the tops of these chimnies caused sad havoc to be done, and the saloon itself has been closed as a consequence.*
>
> *The unroofing also exposed the north and east wings to general and serious leakage, which occasioned heavy damage to furniture, plastering, papering, &c, and has led to a desertion of those portions until repairs can be effected. We are not prepared to give an estimate of the damages, but they must be swelled to a considerable sum.*
>
> *The tin roofing was also blown off, as we have stated, from the large store next to and south of the hotel, occupied by Townsend, Crane & Co. and E.B. Stoddard & Co. Both of these firms had on hand very large stocks of goods that had just been laid in for the fall trade, and both accordingly suffered from the leakage—the former to a considerable extent. We learn also that other houses on Hayne Street have suffered more or less in the rain and storm on Saturday, which marked the clearing off of the gale.*
>
> *Several large houses on East Bay also suffered by the loss or injury to roofs, and the consequent exposure to the violent rains which*

accompanied the storm. Messrs. Cohen & Cohn, R.A. Pringle, McKenzie, Cadow & Co., Chafre, St. Amand, Croft, all suffered, but not, we believe to any serious amount; while Messrs Johnston, Crews & Brawley sustained heavy damages.

The scene on Sullivan's Island, as it has been described in our hearing by many participants, was fearfully sublime. For six successive tides, commencing with the high water of Wednesday morning, there was a gradual accession of the flood, which seemed to be gathering its energies for the final effort of Friday morning. These tides were followed by comparatively slight ebbs, and it was to the warning thus afforded to experienced observers, as well as to the fact that the greatest height occurred in daylight, that we must ascribe the safety of life, as well as the preservation of much that would otherwise have been destroyed. As it is, the character and general aspect of the Island has been so essentially changed, as almost to prevent recognition by any one who should be placed without notice on it.

The shore line has been swept away, together with many of the ramparts, and embankments that had been reared for its security. It is calculated that the general average of surface has been lowered for one foot at least, while in particular instances, there has been a far greater abrasion.

We have already stated the total removal of the old and well known Point House, which had long been a landmark and noted object. The houses near it to the eastward, it is supposed, owed their safety to the bulwark afforded by a large raft of drift matter, composed chiefly of the materials from the Government wharf at Fort Moultrie, which are now strewing the lower end of Middle Street and the space outwards to the creek. The Government wharf has been swept away—and also the Mount Pleasant Ferry wharf, with its house and shed. The communication that has been enjoyed since the disaster, has been kept up by means of the wharf nearest the city, at which is lying the new dredge boat A.H. Bowman, apparently sound in all respects, as was reported by use on Saturday morning.

From the Moultrie House, during the crisis of the gale, the only dry land that could be seen on the Island was the top of the high sand hill East of the Fort. The surf came up unbroken under the house, and for a time broke on the cove or creek side—the spray dashing on the flooring with considerable violence. Two or three of the brick pillars supporting the house were removed, and one was carried by the violence of the shock clear under the house, and now lies embedded in the sand at its rear.

This damage was occasioned principally by the shock received from the heavy timbers on the break-water or wooden rampart before the house, and it was by great exertions and vigilance that greater damages were prevented from this source. The extreme Western end of the piazza has also yielded, and the wooden work in other points betrayed some injuries. The house, generally, stood the severe ordeal beyond the expectations of many who saw the violence and fury of the flood which was assailing its foundations. The roofing in great part was injured or removed, and the interior suffered from the leaks. The house, generally has settled to some extent, and to a greater degree in the centre, but the damages from this source are not definitely ascertained. For some portion of the gale—during its violence—the house afforded welcome shelter to uninvited guests, as for security, it was found necessary to remove all the horses to the livery establishment attached to the piazza of the Northeastern wing.

The old frame work of the Wind Mill, known to all visitors of the house, has been moved for a considerable distance, yielding in various instances to the tide and wind, and finally locating itself where it now stands erect and implanted in the sand. Several of the houses still standing near the Moultrie House, but with a decided inclination towards a downfall, are supposed to owe their partial preservation to the support afforded by faithfully built chiminies in the centre.

The beach row of houses immediately East of the Moultrie House, and known as the Tennessee Row, have been entirely destroyed—some of them not leaving a wreck or vestige to mark their former site, which is now a smooth beach…

The first house observed to yield to the violence of the flood was the one near the Moultrie House to the west belonging to Mr. Owens, but occupied by Hon. W. Izard Bull. Its destruction is described as having been instantaneous almost—those observing it seeing but a slight careening before it was swept away. The houses of Gen. W.E. Martin, H.R. Banks and H. Horlbeck have been all injured seriously and almost equal to a total loss.

Two small houses of Mr. Patterson, have also been swept away. For a considerable distance on towards the Point, but few houses on the beach now are seen without serious injuries, while many have also suffered along Middle Street, and towards the other side. The heaviest damages in many cases were inflicted by floating wrecks and drifts, only those considered the most exposed, yielding to the violence of the water alone. The reach of the waters in covering the Island, was estimated as at least one hundred hands beyond former high tides, which is equivalent to an advance of six feet on ordinary high tides.

At the house of Mr. Kinloch, considered the highest yard or enclosure on all that portion of the Island, the opposing tides met each other.

The fencings, enclosures and the vegetable features of the Island, except the hardy Palmettos, have nearly all suffered, and their ruins add to the general effect of the impression produced by a survey. The tides have not yet receded to their ordinary limits sufficiently to allow of an estimate as to the line that will be adopted—for yesterday and the day before, the whole front appeared a smooth hard beach, to the line up to the fronts of the outer row of houses which had been destroyed in great part as before stated.

The inhabitants of the Island generally speak in warm and grateful terms of the civilities, courtesies and attentions afforded by the officers and garrison of Fort Moultrie, which afforded grateful shelter under the fearful trials of the disaster. At an early hour on Thursday evening, many commenced removal from apprehensions, and even then many were compelled to pass through a considerable depth of the flood, to reach the Fort from their residences. For a portion of Thursday night, however, there was a comparative degree of quiet, which led some to indulge the hope that the worst had been past. The apprehensions of all were renewed, however, at a very early hour on Friday, and the work of preparation began in anxiety and earnestness. All valuables that could be hastily moved were placed as far as possible in security, and the residents repaired to Fort Moultrie and the Presbyterian brick Church. One of our informants estimates that during the height of the storm, there were at least one thousand persons in these two places of refuge.

The scene, in all respects, was one of which no description even by an eye witness could afford an adequate conception to others.

There is nothing, of course, remarkable in the generous aid and courtesies extended by the garrison at Fort Moultrie to the unusual influx of visitors poured in on them by the gale, for it is grateful to reflect that the characteristics of the United States Army would not have authorized any to expect a different result under such circumstances. There was, nevertheless, according to universal consent, a cheerfulness and friendly sympathy of manner and exertion marking the conduct of all, from the officers in command to the privates, which enhanced greatly the effect and value of the relief extended, and which did everything possible to mitigate the inconvenience and discomfort occasioned by the concourse, in a limited space, by so large an assembly, and so large a proportion of females and children. It comes, under these circumstances, at once a duty, and a pleasure to testify to the enthusiastic terms of commendation bestowed by all concerned on the gallant representatives of our Army, and it also affords us in this view much pleasure to record here an authorities expressive of the need of praise that has been justly earned.

By common consent it was decided to hold a meeting of the Island residents, for the purpose of returning thanks to the garrison, and accordingly after due notice, such a meeting took place about half past seven on Saturday the 9th instant, in the Assembly room of the Moultrie House, comprising the guests of that house, and other residents of the Island, who could attend under the circumstances of the case.

These could well be close to the last words of praise to be uttered in Charleston for members of the United States Army for quite some time.

The *Charleston Courier*, on September 12, 1854, reported on the "Loss of the ship *Delia Maria* of this Port."

We regret to learn from Purser F. Dexter of the steamer Gov. Dudley that at 11 o'clock on Monday morning the Dudley fell in with a ship Delia Maria, Captain Pierce…in two and a half fathoms of water, off Hilton head, on the Southern end of Gaston Bank. She had lost her fore, mizzen, main topmast and jib boom. The water was up to her deck on her starboard side and both her anchors were hanging over her bows. Both boats were gone, and there was no sign of her captain, crew or passengers. A Savannah Pilot boat was alongside the ship, the crew of which informed Capt. Crowell of the Dudley, that they had discovered the ship in the situation she then was on Sunday, and that there were several trunks and a quantity of children's clothes on board.

The Delia Maria left Liverpool on the 12th of July for this port, and arrived off our Bar on the 6th just, when she took on board as Pilot Mr. Frederick Burroughs, of this city. Among the passengers were a son of E.W. Walter, Esquire and W.G. Trenholm, Esq. of this city. It is hoped, however, that all on board were able to remain by the ship until the gale abated, in which case they have doubtless reached Hilton Head or some of the neighboring islands in their boats.

The Delia Maria and her cargo were insured in our local offices to the extent of some $60 to $70,000. The remainder, we presume, is insured in New York and England. Her cargo was most valuable.

A search of subsequent editions of the newspaper revealed no further information about the fate of the passengers and crew of the *Delia Maria*. Press reports on September 18 said that

A sudden and brief, but violent tornado or whirlwind, occurred on the Island also at a late hour of Saturday afternoon, which compelled two families to return once more to the temporary shelter of the Fort. The house of the Rev. Paul Trapier was totally unroofed—without injury to the occupants, and the supports of the house of J.S. Heyward, Esq. were so far destroyed as to render it no longer secure. The damage, however, in both cases, may be traced to the effects of the great storm of Friday, which no doubt commenced the work.

The Ferry wharf at Mount Pleasant is partly washed away, so that communication from the boat to the shore is prevented. All the breakwaters, commencing with that in front of the Mount Pleasant Hotel, to the extreme west, are totally wrecked, with the exception of Mr. Moribeck's which being a thick brick wall, is but partially injured...

An arrangement is made to have a flat in attendance at the wharf, to enable passengers &c., to land, until the necessary repairs can be made.

We heard generally that some damages had been sustained on Morris Island on yesterday morning...Every house is reported injured, and some have been utterly destroyed, including that of Mr. Vincent and Mr. Geo Wood, lighthouse keeper. The front beacon has also been overthrown. The Island has been thoroughly flooded and washed... [L]arge sand hills that had afforded considerable protections to points otherwise exposed have been obliterated, and the whole beach side has been completely changed in aspect.

... [S]even or eight houses on James Island have been destroyed. The government wharf also, at the old site of the Fort, has been totally swept away...

Vessels damaged in the storm: The brig Carol; the steamers Mussasoit and G.W. Coffee of the Mt. Pleasant Line; the schooner Rob Roy; the Southerner.

We have heard as yet but dim rumors of the havoc caused on our river plantations by this destructive and fearful gale...

The Nineteenth Century, Part III

From what we have seen and heard, indeed, we entertain the most fearful apprehensions concerning the crops generally of long cottons and rice.

The apprehensions expressed by the newspaper were confirmed in a letter from Laurel Hill, dated September 10, 1854, that was printed in the *Charleston Courier* of September 19, 1854.

I am at a loss how to begin a letter to you. The storm or rather hurricane has ruined everything. All of our rice has been swept away. We had 321 acres cut, and all stacked but 34 acres, when the storm came on us on Thursday night...

All of that rice was destroyed.

It commenced blowing from Northeast on Wednesday and on Thursday we had strong wind from the same quarter, with frequent showers, but with this exception it was not more alarming than on Wednesday. On Thursday night the wind and rain increased, and on Friday the wind still increasing until 12 M, it blew terrific until about night, when it shifted to the East and from that to the Southeast, and continued to blow all night.

At high water on Friday the tide broke over us and...covered the whole plantation and swept everything before it. It came up through the plantations below us from the side, just as a freshet from above, and I have seen no freshet as high since I have been on the [Savannah] River.

The water is still on the fields and perfectly salt. I came down the river this morning from Barnshie landing and water up there in the river is salt. There is not a vestige of rice to be seen anywhere...everything is swept away. On Mr. Manigault's plantation, Mr. Barclay's, Mr. Smith, estate of McPherson, all gone. I have not heard from the estate of Chisolm, but presume they have shared the same fate...

We have three breaks in the river banks but not very deep, which we will mend immediately The tide in the river still continues high, and as soon as the water goes off [we] will save all the rice we can. At the estate of Taylor's we had some 900 acres cut, all of which is gone. Mr. Iszard had some 600 acres, Mr. Smith some 1200 or more. Our peas are all gone...I have never before witnessed such a destruction of timber in the pine land, some places are almost entirely cleared; roads completely barricaded. The loss everywhere is incalculable.

At Laurel Hill Plantation in Beaufort County sixty miles south of Charleston, the plantation was submerged by the roaring tidal surge and the crops ruined.[111] In Georgetown, sixty miles to the north of Charleston, the tide was as high as during the crop killing inundation of 1822.

Adele Petigru Allston of Georgetown described the situation there in a letter to Benjamin Allston on September 20, 1854, this way:

> *Since I wrote you last we have had a great blow, storm. It commenced on the 7th and lasted until the night of the 9th. The tide was higher than has been known since the Storm of 1822. Harvest had just commenced generally and the damage to the crops is immense. From Waverly* [a Plantation on Pawleys Island] *to* [the] *Pee Dee* [River] *on the 8th not one head of rice was seen above the water, not a bank or any appearance of the land was to be seen. It was one rolling dashing sea, and the water was salt as the sea...Many persons had rice cut and stacked in the field, which was all swept away by the flood. Your papa had none exposed in that way for he apprehended high tides from the state of the moon, and prepared as far as possible for it. Mr. J.J. Middleton had 40 acres of very superior rice swept away, a total loss, and many others have suffered in the same way, tho' not to the same extent.*[112]

All in all, a disaster of epic proportions.

The Southeastern states hurricane of 1856

South Carolina's Lowcountry had barely recovered from the devastating storm of 1854 when, two years later, the state's midlands were visited by the remnants of a hurricane that ravaged the Gulf Coast. After savaging shipping in the eastern Gulf of Mexico on August 28 and 29, the storm struck Florida near Panama City, and "raging with unremitting fury,"[113] followed a track across Georgia from that state's southwest corner to the northeast near Augusta.

According to the *Augusta Constitutionalists,*

> *on Sunday, the 31st, about 9 o'clock A.M., the wind being from the northeast, a very heavy rain commenced, and for about twelve hours*

it rained steadily, accompanied with high winds. Such a rain has not descended in this locality within the memory of any of our residents, as far as we could learn…

In every portion of the country we have heard from, the storm has been very disastrous. Every milldam on Butler's, Spirit and Rocky creeks, have given way before the angry floods—the bridges on the common thoroughfares throughout the country, even over the small streams, have either been damaged or carried away.

The center or eye of this storm cut a path between Columbia and Charleston. The streets in both places, and the roads everywhere in between, were strewn with debris. Flooding followed and flowed downstream from the hurricane's course. Timber, crops and fields were drowned or severely wind damaged in a swath that slashed across the midlands, the Pee Dee, eastern North Carolina and southeastern Virginia before the storm made its way out to sea near Norfolk.

By this time in South Carolina's history, the misery caused by tropical cyclones was getting tedious. But Mother Nature being indifferent to the sensitivities or concerns of mankind, there was still much more to come before the close of the nineteenth century and the beginning of the twentieth.

Tragedy on the high seas—the loss of the *Central America*

Unlike today, in 1857, all money issued in the United States was either made of gold or backed by it. By that time, much of the gold came from mines in California. To get it back east, many of those lucky enough to have found it would carry it with them on packet ships from San Francisco to Central America. Having completing this first leg of their adventure, they would traverse the mosquito-infested Isthmus of Panama and, once on the Gulf of Mexico side, board steamers bound for New York. One steamer that regularly made the Caribbean/Atlantic leg of the voyage was the SS *Central America.*

On September 8, 1857, the *Central America* sailed from Havana on the final half of its journey. There were nearly six hundred passengers and crew aboard. The ship was also carrying about twenty-one tons of gold.

The *Central America* and its passengers and crew enjoyed a pleasant cruise toward New York on its first day out of Havana. But on September 9, the ship, its passengers and crew encountered bad weather. By the 10th, the ship found itself in the middle of a hurricane.

Very strong winds were reported along the Carolina coast from Charleston and Georgetown to Wilmington from September 10–13. The weather in Charleston was said to be "stormy" on the 11th. On the 12th, the station at Georgetown reported a "gale" in progress. From this, and what follows, it appears that the hurricane skirted the coastline of both North and South Carolina before disappearing out in the Atlantic.

The *Central America* weathered the storm for several days. From the duration of the ordeal as revealed by those who survived them, it appears that the ship's course matched the path of the storm.

After crashing through heavy seas for three or four days, the *Central America* began to leak. At first well controlled, the incoming seawater soon began flowing into the ship faster than the capacity of the pumps to push it out. Because she was beginning to fill with water, all available members of the crew were put to the task of bailing. When those efforts proved insufficient, male passengers were conscripted into service. Long lines were formed from the interior hull to the deck to pass the buckets back and forth. Some of the women passengers offered to help, but the men refused to allow it.

At some point, the water got as far as the engine room, entered the steam boilers and doused the fires. The ship lost power and, with it, the ability to steer and keep its bow into the waves. At that point, the situation deteriorated severely.

After about a day or more of desperate bailing on the *Central America*, a 120-foot long, two-masted brig named *Marine* appeared in the very troubled waters nearby. It was out of Cardenas, Cuba, and bound for Boston. It was carrying barrels of concentrated molasses. Even though it had lost its flying jib boom, foresails and all its rigging in the storm, its captain, Hiram Burt, had his crew of five intrepid sailors cut away the dragging sails while he valiantly held his ship into the wind.

Meanwhile, back on the *Central America*, its captain recognized the inevitable fate of his ship and made a fateful decision. He gave the order to abandon ship. The ship having insufficient lifeboats, he ordered women and children into lifeboats first.

By this time the *Central America* was listing badly. The only way to get the people into the lifeboats was to lower each one by rope, one at a time, from the upper (and now outer) deck of the ship, all while the oarsmen tried to keep the lifeboats steady and from smashing into the side of the iron mother ship.

Once on the lifeboats, the women, children and oarsmen, all soaked and terrified, made their way through perilous seas to the *Marine*, itself now adrift at a distance of over a mile away, but at least not leaking.

Once aboard the *Marine*, the surviving women and children went to the brig's small cabin. There the women changed their children out of wet clothes and fed and tried to comfort the younger ones. Out of their porthole they could see lights burning on the *Central America*. Many of their husbands and fathers were still on board the imperiled steamer.

The oarsmen who had saved the women and children made trips back and forth between the *Marine* and the *Central America*, ferrying others from one ship to the other. All in all, about six such circuits were made by them during the high seas, pouring rain, flashing lightning and deafening thunder of the storm.

As he approached the *Central America* for the final time, an oarsman named Black was hailed by Captain Herndon and told to stand off. It was too late to save anyone else. Black followed this command.

All throughout the night, the *Central America* had been firing distress rockets. A few minutes after being told to stay away, Black saw a rocket that had been fired from the ship's wheelhouse fly straight out across the ocean. The rocket communicated a clear message: the *Central America* was bow down and sinking.

Black and his men made their way back to the *Marine* for the last time and told the anxious surviving women and children that "The steamer has gone down, and every soul on board of her lost."[114] The survivors wept for their lost loved ones and the other valiant men who died in the fury of the storm.

Captain William Lewis Herndon went down with his ship, joined by most of his crew and nearly all the male passengers. The loss of life totaled around four hundred. Of less value, twenty-one tons of gold went to the bottom at the same time. The loss of gold sparked the Panic of 1857.

The "expedition" storm of 1861

On December 20, 1860, 169 South Carolinians met in Institute Hall in Charleston, and among much fanfare and with great bravado, unleashed the most destructive storm in American history. They voted to secede from the Union.

On January 9, 1861, the United States Navy ship *Star of the West* sailed into the mouth of Charleston Harbor in an effort to re-supply the Federal garrison at Fort Sumter. It was driven off by cannon fire from a battery made up of post-adolescent cadets from the Citadel.

By February 1, 1861, six states in the lower South had joined the madness. This newly formed government demanded that the United

States Army abandon its station at Fort Sumter. Colonel Anderson refused. On April 12, 1861, Anderson was given a final ultimatum: surrender or be fired upon. He refused and, at 4:30 a.m., the bombardment of Fort Sumter commenced. The Civil War had begun.

It took a while for the horrors of war to sink in on the people of both the North and the South. In July, thinking war was a lark, Washington dignitaries took their ladies and picnic lunches to enjoy the battle of Bull Run. Instead of a pleasant afternoon of watching gallant chessboard maneuvering, they all got an eye full of carnage. Terrified, they and their ladies fled back to the nation's capital amidst bloodied, wounded, dying, frightened and defeated Union soldiers.

Insulated by surrounding Confederate states, South Carolina did not experience much bloodshed until the end of the Civil War. During the war's final weeks, General William T. Sherman and his troops took out their anger and feelings of revenge against the midlands as they chased General Johnston to his final capitulation from Georgia to North Carolina.

Although it had a relatively minor role as a battleground, South Carolina was not immune from the tactical maneuvering of war. In an effort to blockade the South and force its submission, the Federal navy posted ships all along the South Carolina coast. They also mounted an assault on Port Royal. That effort was delayed by the "expedition" hurricane of November 1861.

During October of 1861, what was then billed as the largest fleet of war ships ever assembled gathered in the Chesapeake Bay. All totaled, the fleet was made up of seventy-seven warships of various sizes and descriptions. Their purpose was to blockade the South Carolina and Georgia coasts and aid in the seizure of Port Royal, South Carolina. This "expedition" departed on October 29. As this fleet entered the Long Bay of South Carolina on the 30th, "they were swallowed up and spewed everywhere by appalling winds and seas."[115] Waves from the storm were reported to have completely submerged the federally held fort at Cape Hatteras.[116] The transport ship U.S.S. *Governor* sunk off Georgetown. The battery of U.S. Marines on board had to be rescued by the U.S.S. *Sabine.*[117]

The storm scattered and delayed the Federal "expedition" and delayed the assault on Port Royal until after the fleet had a chance to regroup. But they did so relatively quickly.

On November 4, the U.S.S. *Ottawa,* survey ship *Vixen* and the U.S.S. *Seneca* entered Port Royal Sound. They were immediately fired upon by the assembled Confederate naval squadron under the command of Josiah Tatnall. The battle continued until the next day when the U.S.S. *Plembina* and U.S.S. *Pawnee* joined the fight.

On November 7, the Union armada took Fort Walker on Hilton Head and Fort Beauregard on Bay Point. Federal troops landed and seized control of the area. They would maintain that control throughout the war.

On the same day that Forts Walker and Beauregard fell, Robert E. Lee was promoted to full general and placed in command of South Carolina, Georgia and East Florida. He rushed by special train and on horseback toward Port Royal, but it was too late for him to do anything about the situation.[118]

A month or so later, on December 11, 1861, the city of Charleston nearly burned to the ground. The fire started on Bay Street. A cooking fire spread as gale force winds rose and, despite all efforts to extinguish the conflagration, approximately 540 acres of buildings were destroyed.[119]

9.

The Nineteenth Century
Part IV

*And I saw a beast coming out of the sea. He had ten horns and seven heads, with ten
crowns on his horns, and on each head a blasphemous name.*
Revelations 13:1

The 1870s and 1880s

The Charleston area suffered grievously during the 1870s. Sullivan's
Island received the first direct blow of the decade. On August 25, 1871,
the island caught the eye of the storm. The community was engulfed by
a strong storm surge. As the water rose, residents fled to upper floors of
their homes in order to escape. As they did, their houses tumbled under
the force of the water. The inhabitants struggled for their lives. Some
of those inside screamed in terror when their homes were lifted off
their foundations and floated some distance away from where they were
originally situated. Fortunately, no one was killed.

Two years later, on October 16, 1873, another hurricane struck the
Charleston area. With winds out of the southwest at ninety miles per hour,
the maelstrom caused flooding, damage to homes and created a general state
of frightfulness among the population. It totally destroyed the Southeastern
Railroad Depot and the tidal surge lifted railroad cars off their tracks. This
time, the storm took lives.

Two years later, on July 23, 1875, Charleston suffered a catastrophic
fire. Homes, wharves and small vessels all went up in flames as turpentine

running out of one wharf ignited. "The river was on fire for hours," one witness said.[120]

Yet another storm occurred sometime in 1877. The story of it was related most eloquently by Mr. Ben Horry. Mr. Horry lived to be 104 years old. In the 1930s he spoke with an interviewer from the Federal Writers Project about his life. He was then the oldest surviving slave in South Carolina. He toiled on Brookgreen Plantation until freed in 1865.

After emancipation, Ben Horry made his living selling oysters. At one time,

> *I get seventy-five cents a bushel. Now* [during the Great Depression when he was being interviewed], *I satisfy with fifty cents. Tide going out, I go out in a boat with the tide; tide bring me in with sometimes fifteen or twenty bushels. I make white folks a roast; white folks come to Uncle Ben from all over the country—Florence, Dillon, Mullins—every kind of place. Same price roast or raw, fifty cents a bushel.*[121]

When asked about storms, he responded "Storm? Ain't I tell you I been here? Yes sir. More than one storm I live through…Been turn over twice outside there in the sea." Sometime during hurricane season in 1877 (the date was not pinned down during the interview), Ben Horry was casting a seine in the waters of Cape Romaine when a storm struck. "Been rough. Have weather. And breakers take the boat. I swim till I get the rope hold. Two men on the shore have the rope end of the seine rope and I hold on to that end that how I save that time." He then added, "After the weather surrender, we gone back in dere and find cork going up and down and save us net and all."

This storm had struck Georgia and South Carolina and had left seven hundred people dead.

On another occasion, the date of which was unidentified, but most probably August 27, 1881, Ben Horry

> *Had a boat full of people…Wuz Miss Mary, he aunty and the lawyer. I take them fishing outside in ocean. Been in the* [Murrells] *Inlet mouth. Come half way to Drunkin Jack Island. Breaker start to lick the boat. I start to bail. Have maters* [tomato] *can for bail with. And that been dangerous, have too much women in there, they couldn't swim like a man. And it happen by accident when the boat swamp full with water, our feet touch bottom. When he turn over, I did aim to do nothing but swim for myself. Wasn't able to help nobody. But here our feet touch bottom. Only an accident from God.*[122]

The frightening experience caused Mr. Horry to reflect on the frailties of human life and what lies beyond it.

Religion? Reckon Stella [his wife] *got the morest of dat. I sometimes a little quick. Stella, she holds once course. I like a good song. One I like best:*

Try us Lord
And search the ground
Of every sinful heart
What e'er of sin
In us to be found
Oh, bid it all depart![123]

Ben Horry's prayers to the Lord were needed, for just four years later, on August 25, 1885, yet another storm struck. "Great Waves, rolling inward without resistance struck the sea wall of the Battery in swift succession, with a deafening roar, and, bursting into huge water-spouts were hurled against the fronts of residences along the street smashing in windows and doors, leveling fences and inundating the lawns and gardens" is how the *Charleston Yearbook* of 1885 described what happened.

Flood tides from the storm lifted small craft up and over the seawall of the Battery and deposited them on shore next to the houses there. The water reached six feet along the Battery. Boat slips at the foot of King Street were destroyed. The side-wheeler *Alice Clark* was moored at Hamlin's Wharf. It was left listing badly after the storm. The German bark *H. Peters* was dragged a quarter of a mile and came to rest at Bennett's Wharf. Constructed at a cost of $35,000, the boat was so damaged that it sold at auction after the storm for $125.

The "brief respite" of the eye of the storm passed overhead. It "was followed with the tempest swooping down from a new quarter, the west. Though with less force the winds were strong enough to affect serious damage along the Ashley River front. Two sloops lifted up and deposited across Chisolm's Causeway barred wagon traffic there after the waters receded."[124]

The bark *Medbor*, sailing under a Norwegian flag, slipped her anchor at the quarantine station and was driven into Charleston Harbor "like a chip on the surface of a whirlpool." Stripped of rigging, she wrecked near the East Battery. The iron steamer *Glenvilet* was torn from her mooring and collided with the Ashley River Bridge.[125]

The total damage in the city of Charleston was estimated at $2 million. And, once again, Sullivan's Island was left completely under water. All totaled, about twenty-five people died in the storm which, according to one very reliable source, was a category three hurricane.[126]

Then, as if the Lowcountry had not suffered enough, at 9:51 p.m. on August 31, 1886, Charleston and Summerville were struck by a major earthquake. Some ninety-two people lost their lives. Property damage exceeded $5 million. The quake was so strong that it was felt nearly one thousand miles away in LaCrosse, Wisconsin. All total, 2,800,000 square miles were disturbed by this massive movement of the substrata.

The disasters of 1893

The most devastating hurricane season on record to date in South Carolina occurred in 1893. Three storms struck the coast. The first occurred on June 16th. It was bothersome, but memory of it faded in what followed later in the season.

On August 27th a huge tempest made landfall just south of Beaufort. It then followed the curve of the coastline north.

First reports about the storm appeared in the *State* newspaper on August 29, 1893. Communication lines with the rest of the state having been cut during the storm, those reports focused primarily on the damage in the midlands. Those reports were a harbinger of worse to come.

> *This West Indian monster of the air seemed to revel in the destruction it was causing, sweeping with full force over the wooded and gently undulating expanses of the Capital City, neglecting no opportunity of descending upon the prosperity of its frightened inhabitants. It awoke them from their peaceful slumbers with the awful whistle so peculiar to itself and in many instances with the crash of a stately tree, stately no longer but now a ponderous mass of dead weight—through the roofs of their houses.*
>
> *Columbia is as proud of her shade trees as her history and her women. To see hundreds of them pulled up by the roots in every section of the city, thrown across the electric tracks and torn all to pieces was something to sadden the people.*

During the next few days, reports began to arrive in Columbia from elsewhere. Those reports were appalling, including one from the *State* on September 1.

Over three hundred and ninety dead bodies have been found on the islands around Beaufort and Port Royal. Every one of the islands lying around Port Royal and Beaufort are steeped in sorrow. On every door knob here is a bunch of crepe and upon every hillside there are fresh made graves, some already filled, while others are awaiting the bodies that will be deposited in them just as soon as someone can be found to perform the kind Christian act of shoveling the dirt upon the coffin.

The beaches, the undergrowth, trees and shrubbery, the marshes and inlets are turning up new bodies every time an investigation is made. Of the many disasters and devastations which have visited this section of the country, none have been half so horrible as those which came Sunday. Already more than 250 bodies have been found, and those who are all posted around the country and the habits of the people in the storm visited sections are confident in their predictions that the death toll be run as high as 500. Some of the people—and they are among the best people of this section of the State—even place the loss at more than one thousand.

By the time all the bodies were counted, the number totaled more than 2,500.

Houses as much as 20 miles inland were blown away; trees were torn from the earth leaving holes big enough to hide a freight train. Vessels were dashed against the beaches and thrown upon the earth as much as five miles from the water's edge…

Late in the evening the wind took on a great velocity; and as the night advanced the velocity of the wind increased until it attained a speed of 180 miles per hour at 8 o'clock…

These physical features earned the storm the dreaded "category five" classification.

Numerous ships were sunk, damaged or beached in the storm. Among those lost was the steamship *City of Savannah*. Many were rescued at sea by the *City of Birmingham*. Still others who had escaped in lifeboats were plucked from the shores of the Sea Islands by the tugboat *Paulsen*. Some were on Hunting Island. It took those who managed to survive two hours to make their way to the beach through the raging sea and surf. Once near shore they had to struggle through waist deep water for some distance, "holding babies above their heads."[127] Once ashore, they made their way to a lighthouse several miles away, taking shelter there.

Still other survivors off the *City of Savannah* made their way to Coffin Point. From there this latter group of survivors walked a short distance to a nearby house and were taken in by a good Samaritan named Mr. Tripp.

Press accounts of the storm's impact on Charleston were equally grim. Giving a preliminary body count, the news reported that

> *upward of seventy five Negroes were drowned on Warsaw Island. Thirty-one dead bodies have been recovered there, and the corpses are said to be lying around in scores.*
>
> *On the Combahee River on one of the rice plantations a coroner held an inquest on eighty bodies at one time.*
>
> *Of seventy bodies recovered in Coosaw, seven were white people.*
>
> *On Edisto upward of thirty persons were drowned…*
>
> *The death list threatens to assume horrible proportions.*
>
> *The country is so intersected with rivers and there has been such a total destruction of bridges and blockade of roads that there probably never will be any full particulars of this great loss of life. By the time matters resume their normal condition it will be impossible, in such a country, and among such people, to obtain any definite account of the calamity that has befallen them. Those who know where and how those people live can realize how great the loss of life might be in such a storm as that of Sunday.*
>
> *The sea for miles around Charleston bay is filled with dead bodies and wreckage. There are no means of arriving at any reliable account of the casualties at sea.*
>
> *Of the condition of the rice crop it is impossible to speak as yet with accuracy. The estimates of damage vary from 40 to 75 percent. The total crop of Georgia and the plantations on the South Carolina side of the Savannah River might be fairly placed at 500,000 bushels…The crop had already been made and only waited to be marketed.*[128]

The *Columbia Journal* opined that while "the great storm has passed and gone…its effects will be felt in the Palmetto State for the remainder of this year, if not longer. Wreck and ruin have followed in its path everywhere. Dire disaster dawns more and more upon the people as each day passes and they have time to look about them and behold the ruin that has been wrought by the raging winds and surging waters."

In Georgetown at the northern end of the storm's destructive path, there was *an appalling rise in the tide, and the schooners, steamers and small boats along the docks "caught it"—some sinking, some being driven on shore, some bumped and battered out of shape, and others breaking their moorings and being driven along before the gale…*

Immense quantities of wood, barrels, shingles, etc. were swept from the wharves and scattered…some floating up into the streets and some following the current on up the river…

The peninsula, just opposite of [George]*town, is almost a complete wreck. The entire place was under water, the stills were demolished, and most of the property thereon swept away.*

The old City Hall, which has stood for so many years, could not stand the pressure and had to succumb; that is, the sides were blown in, demolishing the clock and leaving the steeple tottering on its four pillars, ready to tumble at any moment.

Many old houses, trees, fences, etc. were blown down and the remaining trees were stripped of all their leaves and most of their branches.

The railroad, country roads, bridges and ferries were in such a condition that the mails could not get out. All the wires are down, and nothing has been heard from the outside world up to this time (Tuesday morning).

The Waverly man boat was unable to get out of the creek mouth on Monday morning, and considerable anxiety was entertained for the residents of Pawleys Island, but the tug Brewster managed to get over to Waverly in the afternoon and ascertained that everybody was still existing…

The rice crop has been damaged extensively…[to such an extent that it] *predicts utter abandonment of rice planting in the future.*

This Editor returned home from Augusta yesterday evening, after a long and circuitous route by way of Columbia, Sumter, Florence and Lanes, by rail hand car and boat.

The damage to the places named is incalculable; ruin and devastation staring us in the face all along the route of travel. Between Florence and Lanes we saw the most water, as well as along the line of the G&W railroad. Travel and telegraph is interrupted all over the country, but from what we could gather the gale was the most severe in years, and crops are almost gone.

We saw people paddling about in boats in several places…The G&W track is washed away and the water is rushing over it in torrents. It will take all of a day at least to repair it.

Several passengers informed us that the old city [of Charleston] *had suffered worse than she did during the cyclone and earthquake periods.*

The tall steeple of the German Church was down as well as others. About 15 houses on Sullivan's Island were blown down and every house on the island damaged.[129]

Chaos ruled after the storm.

Clara Barton, founder of the American Red Cross, came to Beaufort to help after the storm to direct the organization's Sea Island Relief program. She had previously served there in 1863 as a nurse for the Union forces occupying Port Royal.

Ms. Barton's book *A Story of the Red Cross: Glimpses of Field Work* contained the following information about the storm.

The Sea Islands in Beaufort County had about thirty-five thousand inhabitants prior to the storm. Almost all of the residents were black.

Somewhere between four and five thousand Sea Island inhabitants drowned in the storm.

The thirty thousand or so people who survived the storm were left homeless, without food, clothing or shelter. Just about everything had been swept out to sea. Residents described their homes and possessions as "done gone."

A few of the churches, being larger and more strongly built, still remained standing.

During Ms. Barton's first ten days in Beaufort, it was impossible to drive through the principal streets of the town. The refugees there "were a solid moving mass." Those crowding near to the storehouses had to be held back by the police.

The Red Cross closed the storehouses and told the people that all distributions of food and clothing would be made from the islands. Local leaders were appointed to take charge of each community. All clothing and food was consigned to that person to be distributed to each family and person within his charge. The local leader had to account for each distribution as if he were a merchant.

Submerged lands were drained, three hundred miles of ditches were dug and a million feet of lumber purchased and houses were rebuilt. Fields and gardens were planted. All the work was done by the people themselves.

By mid-September, a clearer view of the destruction had been obtained. Upwards of 75 percent of the rice crop had been destroyed. Rice planted in March and April was in bad condition: "wet, tangled, heating both in field stacks and barn yard"[130] as it dried. Much of the rice planted in May was, at the time of the storm, in full bloom and ready for harvesting. Water soaked fields made cutting it impossible. The remainder of that crop that was still in its "milk state" was water soaked and prevented from maturing further.

"Apart from the loss of the crop, the deterioration of the plantation is very great; washed and whipped banks, brakes, &c., &c." is how planter Robert J. Donaldson of Georgetown described the situation.[131]

The storm's damage was not confined to the Lowcountry. According to the *Spartanburg Herald*, "Towards the mountains the rain was very hard and the Broad River, Pacolet and other streams in that neighborhood were out of their banks…and most of the bottom corn left by the former freshet is now gone."[132]

The loss of life in the storm was appalling enough. For those who survived, they assessed their worldly losses. All totaled, those economic damages totaled in the tens of millions of dollars.

The "Flagg storm" of October 1893

Sometime around the end of September 1893, Flora MacDonald LaBruce of Wicklow Hall plantation on the North Santee River had a strange and horrible nightmare. She dreamed that she was standing on a high sand dune at the beach. Below her were mangled children, dead horses and debris from crushed homes. Startled out of her sleep, she told her husband about the dream.

On October 12, 1893, Anna Allston was asleep in her cottage at DeBordieu Beach about twenty miles north of Wicklow Hall in Georgetown County. She dreamed that her father had returned from the dead to warn her to pack her things and leave the island. She told her sister Charlotte of her foreboding and packed her valuables, fearful of what was to come.

Pauline Pyatt was born and toiled in slavery, but lived a long life nonetheless. In 1933, she was interviewed by a writer from the Federal Writers Project about her life. Miss Pyatt had known Dr. Arthur Flagg, a senior warden at All Saints Episcopal Church near Pawleys Island. But Pauline Pyatt knew sixty-five year old Dr. Arthur Flagg a little better than his fellows at the church. Dr. Flagg, it seems, was "a cussing man! All the time cuss!"[133]

On October 12, 1892, Dr. Flagg, his sixty year old and sickly wife Georgianna, their son, Dr. J. Ward Flagg, and three nieces from Summerville were spending time at Dr. Flagg's home on Magnolia Beach in Georgetown County. The nieces were twenty-five-year old Elizabeth Weston, fourteen-year old Pauline Weston and Anne Ward Weston, age at the time unknown. Also present in the Flagg home were their negro servants: Anthony Doctor, Bob Vereen, Bob's wife Barbary, "Maum Peggy," Maum's granddaughters

Adele Myers (wife of Pony Myers), another woman named Clarissa[134] and some others whose names have been lost to history.

A short distance away from Dr. Flagg's beach house was the Flagg's nephew Allard. He was staying at his own house with his son, a servant named Francis Grant and a cat, name unknown.

A little further away were Arthur Flagg Jr., Arthur's wife and their five children Albert, Ward, Eben, Alice and Mattie. The oldest of the children was eleven years of age. The youngest child was still a baby. Mr. and Mrs. Flagg's oldest daughter Madge had recently left to go to school in Georgetown, but Mrs. Flagg's sisters Elizabeth and Alice LaBruce were visiting.

October 12 was a stormy day at Magnolia Beach. The signs were ominous. The tide never went out. Instead of receding, water from the ocean continued to rush into the creeks and marshes throughout the day.

Another warning sign was seen by Cato Singleton and his wife. Former slaves, they were crossing the creek separating Dr. Flagg's home on Magnolia Beach to the mainland after work. They noticed the unusual tide. But they also saw another very eerie phenomenon. The sea was red and yellow and orange as if it was on fire. "That sea made us think of judgment and hell," he later said.[135]

There were also other, more scientific, harbingers of things to come. Among his other possessions, the elder Dr. Flagg kept a "storm ball" (a barometer) at his home. On the twelfth, that instrument "keep a turning round." Adele Myers noticed the changes and "keep telling him [Dr. Arthur Flagg] storm coming. He wouldn't believe 'em. He wouldn't believe."[136]

As it turned out Dr. Flagg's disbelief was not an effective defense against what was coming. Neither were his wealth, social status, position of prominence in his church, any feelings of privilege or entitlement, any belief in his intellectual superiority nor his profane tongue.

The weather continued to deteriorate throughout the day, evening and night of the twelfth. It worsened still more during the early morning hours of October 13, 1893. By this time the winds were blowing furiously. When it became light again, ocean waves were rolling over Magnolia Beach.

The water continued to rise, smashing into everything in its path, including the beach homes.

The elder Dr. Flagg and the others in his home first tried to escape by going to the second floor. The house began to give way. They escaped by climbing out a window onto the piazza roof. It was beginning to break away as everyone climbed onto it. The roof broke lose and began to float with the surging tide. As it passed a large sea cedar tree, those on the roof grabbed on to its branches and hung on for their lives.

Annie Weston was knocked off the limb she was clutching on two separate occasions, but managed to pull herself back "in spite of floating boards, furious sea and sand-laden winds cutting flesh like sharp pieces of glass."[137] Exhausted, she was about to give up her fight when Dr. Flagg told her to "Live for your mother's sake."

Shortly thereafter, the "forty-foot waves…claimed Dr. Arthur Flagg, his wife, and Elizabeth and Pauline Weston. Each one left fighting his own fight, and was cruelly beaten by the waves."[138] The same fate awaited the servants, Anthony Doctor, Bob and Barbary Vereen, Maum Peggy, Adele Myers, Clarissa and the others.

Only Annie Weston survived to tell what happened.

Meanwhile, the home of Arthur Flagg Jr. and everyone in it died in the storm. No one survived to detail the last hours and moments of the lives of the members of this family.

Elsewhere, Allard Flagg, his son, servant and cat jumped onto the roof of the kitchen as it floated by. They were carried by the current to the mainland near his winter home, the Hermitage.

John Dozier was at Ocean View, near Magnolia Beach, about two miles across the marsh from the ocean. When he realized the storm was getting bad, he left his house to turn his horses loose. When he left his house, the ground was damp with rain. Upon his return about twenty minutes later, the rising water was all around him. He later said that it was like a tidal wave overtaking him. He hurriedly got his wife and the rest of his family into two small boats and evacuated to a safer place.

"Previous to the storm, there were sand hills in front of his house, ten or twelve feet high. Now there are none, and an almost unobstructed view of the ocean may be had. His house is a complete wreck," is how the Georgetown newspaper of October 18 described the results of the storm at Ocean View.

A little further to the south, at Pawleys Island, by the grace of God no lives were lost. Nonetheless, "everything belonging to our friend Mr. Frazier, from Pee Dee, was swept away, while they escaped almost miraculously, with their lives, by taking refuge on a mound, I may say, of sand, in the wind and rain, which were simply awful. Dr. Tucker's house was also carried off, with everything this family owned."[139]

On October 13, 1893, Pauline Tucker LaBruce wrote to her sister Annie Tucker, who was at a seminary in Clinton, South Carolina, about what had just been experienced on Pawleys Island. At the time she wrote the letter, she was still unaware of what had happened at Magnolia Beach a short distance to the north.

In her letter, "Poodie" LaBruce told her sister that the weather had been bad for more than a day, but then at about two o'clock in the early morning of the 13th,

> *the wind rose and I left my room and came with Mama in Mattie's room and John stayed in our room. We got up about half past seven and the creek tide was rising high then but never reached its height until ten o'clock and such a tide I pray I may never see or hear of again...*[with the] *ocean and creek meeting and rushing across* [which] *just swept the houses away and thank God it was daylight for if it had been last night God only knows what would have happened in the darkness and terror of the night!*
>
> *It happened about half past nine or ten o'clock this morning and David's house went first, then Lulie saw our house split apart at the ridge boards. The next minute she looked and it had been washed away; not a sign of a brick or board or anything, and the ocean and creek a-surging in between. Then the waves washed through the Fraser's piazza. Then a tremendous wave rushed through the dining room. Then they* [the Fraser's: Mr. Fraser, Lulie, Josie, Pauline, Alice, Bennie, Cousin Lucy and the servants] *left the house and got up on a high hill at the back of the house...*[A]*nd then that house caved in and was carried right out.*
>
> *Darling, imagine their feelings on that hill, the creek washing up at the back, the ocean at the front and the sand crumbling and falling in all the time! And if the tide had risen for ten minutes longer, all would have been lost...*
>
> *Plenty of chickens, etc. drowned and hundreds of little sparrows driven inland by the storm and all flying about and some got drowned, but not many. O, this is a storm never to be forgotten.*[140]

A little further south, at South Island, Captain Henry Williams of the schooner *Encore* took a rowboat with two women across the inlet to Debordieu beach the day before the full brunt of the storm struck. "Miss Mary" was clutching her black cat in her lap. Her female companion urged her to throw the cat overboard, fearing it would bring bad luck. "But [Miss Mary] held the cat, if anything, more tenderly. And I had my pet Italian Greyhound in my lap, carefully covered up as he was timid. Our boat pitched and rolled over those breakers from the Atlantic and I hope never to experience again!" the letter's author wrote.[141]

Worse was to come.

After walking about a mile to the home of Aunt Charlotte and Anna Allston, the letter writer sat with the others and talked about the weather. Then she and Aunt Charlotte went for a walk on the beach, "but it was blowing such a gale there was no pleasure in walking." They passed a ship that had been blown ashore during the August hurricane.

Upon return to the house, Anna Allston told of the dream in which her father had told her to leave the island. Aunt Charlotte responded, "Oh Annette, you and your dreams!"

On the morning of the thirteenth, one of the servants came running into the bedroom and said "Gracious God, Missy, you and Miss Mary there in bed taking it so easy! You don't see how the breakers are breaking over the ship on the beach?" The two women rushed to their window "and sure enough, the breakers were mountain high, so we decided to get up."

The general excitement mounted when someone noticed that one of the servants was missing. When reassured that he had simply gone to retrieve his fish net,

> *two goats came butting against the front door and "baa-ing." I wanted to let them in but Aunt Anna said, "If you open that door we are all gone!" I was frantic and prayed that* [the goats] *would drown quickly.*
>
> *Nannie went into our room, fell into a rocker and tried to faint. Auntie rushed up to her and while shaking her finger at her said "Nannie behave yourself. Remember you are a woman and get up and help! Nobody has time to faint now." It acted like magic and Nannie was all right after that.*
>
> *We got on our bed to get out of water. Nannie took her child and father, Daddy Cuffie, into her room, the "storm room." Aunt Anna opened the Prayer Book and handed it to Auntie and said "My daughter, read the prayer for those at sea."*

At that point, a tree crashed through the front door on the waves and water rushed into the house. It rose to waist deep. The women fled for the storm room, the stronger, higher, well-anchored add-on to the house that had been built after the hurricane of 1822. But even in that higher refuge the water rose to the height of several feet.

While huddled together in the storm room, the occupants could hear the ocean's waves breaking on the roof. Then they heard a loud crack as if the room was about to break away. One of the women said, "If it cracks again, we will be gone!" The same Nannie who was prepared to faint a short time ago replied "Miss, don't be afraid. Master Jesus is at the helm."

Nannie's faith was rewarded. The water ebbed. The storm's fury started to abate. A bird flew into the window of the storm room and was caught by one of the children who gently set it down. Then another flew in and came to a rest. The survivors took it as a sign, like Noah's doves, that the danger was over.

> The water gathered around us
> We trembled in the gale
> For we thought every moment
> That human strength must fail
>
> We could only look to Jesus
> Pleading looks we gave
> And the Blessed Master
> In mercy stooped to save
> *-Survivor's poem*

Those left behind by the Allstons on South Island did not fare well either. The island had been severely damaged in the August storm, but the "brave little band of inhabitants gathered up their fragments, and with renewed energy in part restored their homes."[142] But then, on October 12 and 13, their tiny community was again visited by nature's ravages.

> *The severity of this storm and its damage has never been equaled, not even by those of 1854 or 1822. Our high dry island, covered with huge oaks and lovely palmettos interspersed here and there with once lovely cottages, today is a sad spectacle, houses swept away, trunks, bedding, clothing and food swallowed up by the huge billows of Winyah Bay. Many families tonight have no roof of their own to cover their heads…*
>
> *Had the tide and wind lasted one hour longer, I doubt if a single soul would have been left alive to tell of our sad disaster.*[143]

According to the *Georgetown Times* of October 18, 1893, about forty lives were lost on South Island.

The next few days were devoted to recovering bodies. Ben Horry, then in his sixties, helped with the search. During the storm he was on a steamer boat that had left Charleston at 5:00 a.m. The trip to Georgetown, through very rough seas, took until 9:00 p.m. On the way he helped rescue a married couple and two children in a small boat. They had tied themselves to the mast of their vessel so they would not be washed overboard. "After that they quit call me Ben; they call me Rooster," he later crowed.[144]

> *After Flagg storm, Colonel Ward take me and Peter Car, us two and a horse, take that shore* [followed the shore line] *to Little River. Search for all them what been drowned…Find dead horse, cow, ox, turkey, fowl—everything. Gracious God! Don't want to see no more thing like that. But no dead body find on beach outside Flagg family. Find two of them chillun way down to Dick Pond what drowned to Magnolia Beach; find them in a distance apart from here to that house. Couldn't 'dentify wedder Miss or who…All that family down out because they wouldn't go to this lady house on higher ground.* [Old Doctor Flagg] *wouldn't let none of the rest go. Servant all drown. Betsy, Kit, Mom, Adele. Couldn't 'dentify who lost from who save till next morning. Find old Doctor body by he vest stick out of the mud; fetch doctor body to shore and he watch still ticking.*

The bodies of Mattie Flagg's infant daughter and that of her sister were found along the shore at Debordieu. From the positions of the bodies, it appeared that Ms. Flagg had held the baby tight to her breast throughout their ordeal. The two bodies were found next to each other, with Ms. Flagg's arm outstretched and the baby at the tip of her fingers. Those who found them said it looked as if the baby had rolled out of Ms. Flagg's arm as the receding water departed.

All totaled, this horrible storm killed some three thousand people between Puerto Rico and the Carolinas.

10.

The Twentieth Century

God is our refuge and strength…we will not fear though the earth give way…though its
waters roar and foam and the mountains quake with their surging.
Psalm 46: 1–3

The twentieth century brought a lull in storm activity to South Carolina. According to NOAA records, four storms made landfall during the century's first twenty years. Two were category one storms, one was a category two and the other a category three. Of these, the storm of August 27, 1911, was historically the most significant. It left seventeen people dead. Its winds were clocked at 105 miles per hour.

The stormy Atlantic had brought rice to South Carolina in 1685 when a brigantine fled to the safety of Charleston harbor from a storm. The ship's captain, John Thurber, gave less than a bushel of seed rice from Madagascar to Dr. Henry Woodward in gratitude for assistance while in Charleston.

According to Merle Shepard, entomologist and former resident director at Clemson University's Coastal Research and Education Center, "Woodward planted the seed and spread the rice to other farmers. Within a few years Lowcountry growers were exporting the rice to the other colonies and to Europe. It eventually became known as Carolina Gold,"[145] a name matched by the color of the grain.

What the sea had brought, the sea took away. Rice planting had been very heavily dependent on slave labor. With the abolition of slavery, rice harvests began to decline. The storms of 1893 severely damaged the rice fields, inundating them with brackish water and causing the earthen impoundments to the fields to collapse. The storm of 1911 dealt the final blow, damaging the relatively few remaining rice fields so badly that it was no longer economical to try to cultivate that crop. As a result, Carolina Gold ceased to exist—it did, that is, until 1986 when fourteen pounds of it were given to the owners of Turnbridge Plantation near Bluffton to plant. The number of locations and the quantity of rice under cultivation has been increasing ever since.

Rice was not the only industry to suffer in the 1911 storm. Around the turn of the century, a new business had taken hold in Georgetown. Atlantic Coast Lumber Company (ACL) opened its doors to capitalize on the area's vast timber resources and its large, and largely unemployed, black work force. ACL soon became the largest lumber mill on the Atlantic coast. It was soon joined by the Winyah Lumber Company, the Palmetto Lumber Company and other smaller mills.

All of Georgetown's lumber industries were seriously harmed in the 1911 storm. But the "damage to the mills [was] insignificant compared to the loss of timber in the woods."[146]

In the city of Georgetown, wharves and the ships tied to them were banged about. Riverfront stores and warehouses were flooded and their contents damaged or destroyed. The storm left the area's economy reeling.[147]

Only one storm struck during the next twenty years. It made landfall on August 11, 1940, near Beaufort. It was a category two storm when it struck, causing the same sort of de-roofing of houses, crops damage, livestock deaths and timber destruction that, by now, had come to be expected. Throughout its brief meteorological life, this storm claimed fifty human lives, but none in South Carolina.

The period between 1941 and 1960 was also relatively quiet. A total of five storms struck South Carolina. Three were small category one storms. Another reached category two. The third was a category three hurricane when it struck South Carolina. Of these tropical cyclones, the two most memorable were Hurricane Hazel and Hurricane Gracie. They struck at opposite ends of the coast.

Hazel—1954

Hurricane Hazel killed nearly one thousand people in Haiti before making its way past the Bahamas to the Carolina coast. Its maximum sustained winds there were 150 miles per hour, making it a category four storm.

When she arrived along South Carolina's coast on October 15, 1954, Hazel brought a storm surge of 14.5 feet with it. The wind and waves pulverized the beaches of the northern coast from Pawleys Island to Little River. Her winds were clocked at 125 miles per hour when she actually made landfall near the North Carolina border.

At Pawleys Island, homes were left in shambles. Windy Hill Beach, north of Myrtle Beach, was demolished. "Not a single structure was left standing"[148] at Windy Hill. Only two of 275 buildings were left standing at Garden City, south of Myrtle Beach.

The *State* newspaper reported,

> *Myrtle, caught in the swirl of mountainous waves that reached as high as 40 feet, sustained heavy damage. Myrtle Beach, the biggest and brightest in the resort chain, lost its front beach, the ocean-front row of cottages. Those on the second row, across the ocean boulevard, were damaged in various degrees. Tin roofing was wrapped across facades of some of the houses like tissue paper…*
>
> *Sections of the boardwalk were ripped up all along the beaches and lay in crazy patterns, tilted against sagging porches of houses on the second row…*
>
> *Mayor Ernest Williams of Myrtle Beach estimated damage in this area alone at five million dollars.*
>
> *I don't think a single building along Ocean Boulevard on the waterfront escaped damage, and a lot in the west were damaged too…*
>
> *"[Waves] would break over the top of a house, and that house wasn't there any more,"*

the mayor told reporters.

The Second Avenue pier and the Ocean Plaza pier at Myrtle Beach were destroyed.

A total of 273 houses were destroyed in Myrtle Beach. That represented about 80 percent of the oceanfront and adjacent structures. Ocean Drive lost 450 houses. Crescent Beach lost 200. Cherry Grove Beach lost 300 out of its 450 houses.[149]

At Pawleys Island, a fire followed the storm. It destroyed about forty houses.

"Pawleys was unrecognizable to those who knew it. The ocean had cut new channels straight through the island to the marsh behind, splitting the inland into a number of smaller ones." The newly constructed pier at Pawleys Island was heavily damaged. About seven hundred feet of the eight hundred-foot long structure were swept away in the storm. High, protective sand dunes were washed away.

In Georgetown, Benjamin Johnson was hit by a falling tree. His leg and spine were fractured.

Hazel killed ninety-five people and did $281 million dollars ($1.94 billion in 2005 dollars) in damage in the United States. Twenty people were dead or missing in the Carolinas. One was from South Carolina.

Hazel was a very fast-moving storm. Her forward motion averaged around thirty-two miles per hour. The combination of high winds and swift forward movement proved to be a deadly combination. Where other storms tend to lose strength once they hit land, Hurricane Hazel remained a "bulldozer storm"—it maintained a great deal of its strength as it raced inland.

Hazel was still a category three storm when it passed over Raleigh, North Carolina. Wind gusts of 113 miles per hour were felt in New York City, even though that metropolis is about 700 miles further north and, during Hazel, was nearly 150 miles east of the storm's path. Hazel's winds were clocked at over 100 miles per hour as it passed through upstate New York. It produced record flooding all along its path and well into Canada, where it dropped eight and a half inches of rain and its winds were still blowing at 90 miles per hour. Hazel killed another eighty-one people in Canada, including five firemen who died in rescue attempts and thirty-two sleeping residents drowned by a flash flood in the Humber River. Some two thousand families were left homeless in Canada by Hurricane Hazel, making her one of the worst natural disasters in that nation's history.

Hurricane Gracie—1959

Hurricanes Connie and Diane skirted Georgetown and Horry Counties in late August 1955, causing minor damage. Then, on July 9, 1959, a category one storm with winds of seventy-five miles per hour came in from the southeast. That storm was just a small taste of what was to follow.

On Tuesday, October 1, 1959, Hurricane Gracie hit Beaufort County. With a barometric pressure of 28.05 inches (950 Mb) and sustained winds of 120 miles per hour, this fast moving storm held Beaufort in a "four hour reign of terror."[150] With gusts up to 138 miles per hour, the storm killed four people and damaged 2,394 area homes. The storm also sunk twelve shrimp boats.

As bad as it was, ninety-six-year old John Grayson, a survivor of the killer hurricane of August 1893, later told a reporter from the *Beaufort Gazette* on October 29, 1959, that Gracie was "not too big a storm." Mr. Grayson recalled the storm surge that had brought so much death and destruction to the Sea Islands in the earlier storm. While Gracie had very high winds, perhaps even higher than the killer storm of 1893, it struck on a low tide and did not carry water inland like its predecessor had sixty-six years earlier.

Gracie raced into South Carolina, crossed over Columbia and entered North Carolina near Charlotte. After looping through western Virginia, West Virginia, Pennsylvania and lower New York State, she exited again into the Atlantic by dissecting Connecticut.

The years 1961 to 1980 were the dullest on record in South Carolina as far as hurricanes are concerned. Only one storm, David in 1979, had been a hurricane before hitting Beaufort. Although it struck on high tide, its winds were below hurricane strength when it made landfall, so its impact was small. The storm tracked inland over Columbia and Rock Hill before heading overland to Nova Scotia. It dumped a lot of rain, but no lives were lost and damage was comparatively minor.

Despite the lack of storm activity, this same period of time is significant nonetheless, for it corresponds with a surge in building of new housing and resorts of various types along South Carolina's coast. New high-rise hotels sprung up along the state's northern beaches. Luxury homes and condominiums were built on Sea Islands south of Charleston. Housing and resort development boomed on Hilton Head Island and its surroundings as "heirs property" (land to which legal ownership had been passed from generation to generation of the indigenous black population) was gobbled up by developers in lawsuits to partition the land.

The scheme was simple: South Carolina law provides that when a person dies without having written a will, his or her property is to be divided between the closest blood kin. As an example, if a man with a wife and two children dies, his property (including any land) is divided equally between his three survivors. If there is no spouse, the surviving children divide the property equally. If there is no spouse or children, the parents of the deceased share in the estate. In their absence, siblings share, and so on.

When land passes in this way from generation to generation, title to it becomes divided and re-divided in a tangle of family members, some close and some very remote. While some may continue to live on the land, their co-tenants or co-owners still retain "an undivided interest in the entirety" of the property. This means that each co-owner can use and enjoy the entire property, but, at the same time, cannot exclude any of the others from the use and enjoyment of the land. Importantly, each individual co-tenant retains the legal right to sell or otherwise transfer his or her fractional interest in the property to a third party.

Heirs property is relatively easy to identify on tax rolls. The words "Heirs of...c/o..." customarily appear on those lists as the way of identifying the recipient of the annual property tax bill. The location of heirs property is equally easy to identify by reference to tax maps.

When a piece of heirs property is sited at a desirable location, all anyone has to do is to make some inquiries and locate one of the co-owners and buy that person's share. While the existence of a family feud can make this task easier, even in the absence of one the process is not that hard. Greed has been a great motivator throughout history. Even more innocently, to a working mom living far away who has lost all contact with other members of her extended family, an offer of several thousand dollars to sign a deed to property she otherwise had no knowledge of can be much needed "found money." To her distant kin living on the property, it is legal trouble which ultimately results in their being forced off their land.

Once a fractional interest in the land is purchased, a "partition" action is brought by the new co-tenant. It does not matter how small the fraction of ownership that was acquired. It could be a 1/100th interest or even smaller. As a co-tenant, this new co-owner shares equal legal rights with everyone else. In order to realize a profit from his ownership interests, he can commence an action to divide and sell the property.

This interloper is usually a straw man for a developer. The lawsuit names the other known heirs by name as defendants and they are served with a summons and complaint. The lawsuit also names "John Doe" as a defendant. That name is used to identify any other heirs whose identities are unknown to the new purchaser. He is then served "by publication": an ad printed in very tiny type at the back of a designated newspaper appears one time each week for three weeks. A friendly (from the developer's point of view) local attorney is appointed by the court to represent "John Doe."

Once everyone is served (including "John Doe") and the time to file responsive pleadings has elapsed, a hearing is set. The customary result of the hearing is an order for the sale of the property from the courthouse steps and a division of the proceeds of the sale among the heirs. The division is done *pro rata*—divided in fractions equaling the percentage of ownership of each co-owner.

On sale day, the developer or his agent stands on the courthouse steps and bids. While the successful bidder is the one who offers the most money, bidders traditionally are bargain hunters and land sold in this way typically sells for much less than it is actually worth.

Titles to much of the land on Hilton Head and adjoining Sea Islands passed from the hands of black families into the hands of wealthy individuals and corporations in this way between 1961 and 1980. Many people were ousted from what had been family farms and homesteads where their ancestors are buried—including those who drowned in earlier storms. Hotels, homes and condominiums sprung up. The well heeled moved in as those down-in-the-heels were pushed out. Much of what has just been described occurred during the decades-long lull in hurricane activity of the twentieth century.

1989—Hazel's son Hugo

A long storm lull ended abruptly in September of 1989. Beginning its life as Tropical Depression 11 in the southern Atlantic, a growing mass of bad weather crossed the southern Atlantic and became a hurricane when it was about seven hundred miles east of Barbados. It was given the name Hugo.

The island of Guadeloupe was the first to feel Hugo's wrath. With winds of 130 miles per hour, a ten-foot tidal surge and dumping fifteen inches of rain, Hugo left five dead, eighty injured and more than ten thousand people without a home.

Hugo next struck the Virgin Islands, killing nine and leaving a path of destruction in its wake. Then, in Puerto Rico, it dumped nearly twenty inches of rain, causing flooding and mudslides everywhere.

When Hugo reached the Bahamas, the people in South Carolina began to take closer note of the storm. At that point its winds were clocked at 105 miles per hour and it was moving across the Atlantic at 12 nautical miles per hour.

A hurricane warning went up in South Carolina on September 20th as the storm wobbled at sea, gaining strength. Public officials warned people to get out of the way of the growing menace.

Heavy rain and gusting winds invaded the Charleston area in the early morning hours of Thursday, September 21. Roads became clogged as evacuees from Daufuskie Island in the south to Myrtle Beach in the north began to move inland. Roads were so clogged in some areas that it took as much as eight hours to make the two hour drive from Charleston to Columbia on the interstate highway connecting those two cities.

In the late afternoon, a tornado touched down in Myrtle Beach. Its appearance heightened tensions there.

Hugo's winds kept increasing. As it began to get dark outside, the storm's winds had increased to 135 miles per hour. It was now a category four storm. At this point in time, Hugo was still wobbling, so it remained uncertain exactly where the storm would make landfall.

At 9:00 p.m., the clock on Saint Michael's Episcopal Church at the "four corners of the law" in Charleston stopped ticking, as if time and God were holding their breath.

At 11:00 p.m., Hugo came roaring ashore. Its eye passed just to the north of Charleston at the Isle of Palms and Sullivan's Island. Force four winds, accompanied by a twenty foot storm surge came roaring ashore, demolishing houses and, in some cases, burying inhabitants in the debris, some alive and some not.

In Charleston, a radio tower and several trees fell onto the county's Emergency Preparedness Center. The 150 people inside had to run for cover. The roof at city hall peeled back, leaving the mayor and his staff exposed to the storm. The headquarters of the Charleston Police Department began to cave in. All around the area, the windows of cars exploded because of the dramatic drop in barometric pressure. The steeples at the Blessed Sacrament Roman Catholic Church on Highway 17 South fell over. At the Medical University (MUSC), hospital staff scrambled to move desperately ill patients away from windows and to attend those who were gravely ill or seriously injured.

At nearby Roper Hospital, the emergency generators powering vital equipment began to fail. Lines leading from fuel tanks outside had been damaged, so fuel had to be pumped by hand from the tanks to the generators. That meant that hospital maintenance staff had to go outside into the fury of the storm to do the pumping. Daniel Dyer and David Johns did just that. With ropes tied around them and the clothes they were wearing as their only protection, the two men ventured through water that was up to their waists. They took turns hand pumping the fuel, one pumping away while the other looked out for flying debris. Together, they kept critical care units running throughout the horrifying hours that followed.

Meanwhile, inside MUSC, two preschoolers were sitting fretfully inside a room when its windows were sucked out by the storm. Nurse Patti Pipkin grabbed the children and tried to pull them out the door into the hall. The suction was so strong that it pulled the children back toward the window where death from a horrible fall awaited. Nurse Pipkin held on. As she did, the door slammed shut on her arm. She continued to hold tight to the children anyway. Doctors standing nearby came to her aid and she, along with the children, were pulled to safety.

At Charleston Memorial Hospital, a short circuit caused emergency generators to shut down. Russell Minter and Glenn Pack crawled out on the building's roof during the height of the storm to get the generators running again. When they did, each was tossed by the wind and they were almost blown off the roof. But each struggled against the wind and, amid the flying debris, got the generators started. The generators kept running for the rest of the storm, keeping respirators, incubators and a host of other life preserving and life saving machinery in operation.

When the eye of the storm arrived, several Charleston firefighters attempted to free people who had been trapped inside houses that had collapsed on Sires Street, Moultrie Street and Perry Street. Arthur McCloud, the man under the debris at the Sires Street location, could not be freed until the next morning. He died sometime later, his final hours having been a nightmare of wind, rain and pain. But at least he had the solace of reassuring words of those who were trying to save him.

All totaled, some thirty buildings in Charleston collapsed completely. A nine-story condominium complex was also destroyed.

The Ben Sawyer Bridge connecting Sullivan's Island to the mainland was twisted and upended. Sullivan's Island and the Isle of Palms were left in shambles.

On Johns Island, the walls of an emergency shelter nearly collapsed, terrifying the people inside.

On the Ashley, Cooper and Wando rivers, many boat owners sought to ride out the storm on their vessels. Two men who stayed on a shrimp boat were killed when their vessel was tossed against the Highway 41 bridge and dashed to pieces. Another man who stayed on his cabin cruiser was hurled into the water when the boat broke to pieces in the storm. He awoke the next morning afloat on two life jackets that had been tied together. The bodies of the two shrimpers who had drowned were a few feet away in the marsh.

A couple from Florida attempted to keep their catamaran afloat. They drowned. So did a thirty-year old Charleston man who had tried to keep his thirty-foot powerboat from sinking.

In St. Stephen, about forty-five miles inland, a middle-aged couple fled their mobile home for the perceived safety of their car nearby. The wife was killed when another mobile home was tossed onto the car.[151]

The strongest quadrant of any hurricane is on the right-hand, or northeastern, side of its eye. Rotating counterclockwise, this is the part of the storm that has spent the most time over warm water before hitting land. In the case of Hurricane Hugo, this most deadly part of the storm struck the community of Awendaw, the Francis Marion National Forest and the town of McClellanville to the north of Charleston.

Tales of horror abound from these communities to the north. One husband and wife decided to ride out the storm with their pets at home on Bull's Bay. Their home was eighteen feet above sea level, so they thought they were safe. They ended up standing on chairs in a small room in the upper half of their split-level house to keep their heads above water. They remained there gasping for breath until the water receded.

At Lincoln High School in McClellanville, about 1,100 people sought refuge in what had been designated by emergency preparedness officials as a shelter. Although the planners thought the building was twenty feet above sea level, in truth the elevation was only half as high.

As the extent of the storm's fury started to become apparent, many area residents went to the high school. At first, everything was fine— or as good as could be expected when staying at a shelter during a hurricane. Then the lights went out. Fear began to spread, but was eased when emergency lights in the hallway came on. Then those went out too, leaving everyone to face the eerie sounds of the wind in near total darkness.

Then events began to develop quickly. Water came seeping in under doors and through ventilation openings. Those who could see outside saw dark waters swirling and rising, trapping people inside. Pretty soon the water levels between the inside and outside equalized, but not before the water was waist deep or higher. As the water rose, people had to climb up on desks and chairs to keep their heads above water. Frightened parents pushed ceiling tiles aside and held their children in the air. Others parents climbed out windows, pulling their children up with them on to the roof of the school. Once there, everyone who escaped floodwaters this way was exposed to the full fury of the storm.

After several hours of terror, the water finally receded in apparent answer to the frantic cries and prayers of those who had fled to the school for shelter.

Elsewhere in McClellanville and neighboring Awendaw, homes and other buildings were inundated, knocked from their foundations and destroyed. The Francis Marion National Forest was leveled by the storm. Tens of thousands of huge trees snapped like toothpicks. Wildlife of all kinds died in the thousands and thousands.

Back in McClellanville, one family that remained behind had to scramble into the attic of their one story home as the tidal surge came roaring in. As the water continued to rise, the father broke a hole in the roof to avoid drowning. As the situation became even more desperate, he pulled wire loose from inside the attic and used it to tie all the members of his family together. He later said that he did that because he wanted their bodies to be found together after the storm.

Further to the north, at Pawleys Island and the surrounding beach communities, the destruction was widespread. Beach homes were washed away, some into the sea and others into the marshes behind the barrier islands. New creek channels were cut inland. Old, high protective sand dunes were washed away.

In Garden City, 90 percent of the homes were destroyed. In Surfside Beach, 150 oceanfront buildings were declared to be unsafe. In Myrtle Beach, 14 motels were no longer suitable for trysts because of the twisting winds.

Inland in Williamsburg, Clarendon and Sumter counties, homes were crushed by falling trees, cars were overturned and streets and roads were rendered impassable by debris and trees lying everywhere.

In Florence County, some people who had fled there for safety were shocked when the roof of the motel in which they were staying blew off.

Electricity failed everywhere. Telephone lines were down. Many people lost water service because of the storm. With a few exceptions, radio and television stations were knocked out of service.

The effects of Hugo have been variously described by different people as "looking like an atom bomb had gone off" or "the end of the world" or, simply, "heartbreaking" or "horrible." All totaled, Hugo caused some $7.1 billion dollars ($10.9 billion in 2006 dollars) in damage in the Carolinas. Worse, Hugo was a killer. In addition to the human lives it took in the tropics, it killed fifty-seven people on the United States mainland, thirty-five of whom were in South Carolina. Six people drowned. Seven were crushed. Sixteen people died in fires. Others were killed by falling trees or by electrocution.[152]

One legend told about Hurricane Hugo involves a man who was sitting on his porch as the wind began blowing, rocking in his chair. A deputy sheriff came by in a patrol car and warned that a storm was coming and told the man to evacuate. The man responded "I have faith in God. He will look out for me."

As the storm worsened and the water rose, the same deputy came back in a boat and invited the man to get in, warning of impending danger. The man refused, again responding, "God will look out for me."

The storm surge struck and the man retreated to the roof of his house. The same deputy hovered above in a helicopter, shouting for the man to get into the rescue basket. The man refused, once again responding, "God will look out for me."

The man drowned in the storm. When he reached the Pearly Gates, he had a bewildered look on his face. He said to Saint Peter, "What happened? I had faith. Why didn't God protect me?" Saint Peter answered "We sent a car, a boat and a helicopter, what more did you expect?"

Over the last sixty-five years, three storms (Hurricanes Hazel, Gracie and Hugo) were big enough to make a lasting impression on those who lived through them. It is fair to say that those three maelstroms now form the living memory of coastal inhabitants. Hazel struck along the northern coast in 1954, Gracie struck the southern coast in 1959, and Hugo struck in the middle in 1989. Only longtime residents will remember Hazel or Gracie, and then only depending on where they lived at the time. Hugo struck more than fifteen years ago, so even Hugo may not be in the minds of many of those who have migrated to South Carolina since. Indeed, all some residents may remember about the danger of a hurricane is the inconvenience suffered when evacuating for a storm that never struck. That's not good. Like the villagers in the town where the little boy cried wolf, some people may now be disinclined to heed storm warnings or to fully appreciate the danger from the sea. In point of fact, that beautiful, warm ocean water that has attracted so many to its shores is not as benign as it seems.

To those who lived through it, Hurricane Hugo was a nightmare. However, according to one prominent South Carolina climatologist, Hugo was "a wimp in the history of Charleston…as far as major hurricanes go. It largely ate pine trees that should never have been planted in the first place…[a]nd lots of structures that should never have been built where they were built."[153] While this sort of statement might easily be dismissed coming from an ordinary person, coming as it did as a public statement by a well-known South Carolina scientist, it is chilling indeed.

If this expert assessment is correct and Hugo was a "wimp," much worse can be expected in the future. That being the case, it does not take an expert to figure out what to do when each future storm approaches. As one elderly woman told a television reporter after experiencing Hugo's horrors, she believed that it was wisest to "evaporate" the next time a hurricane warning was issued.[154]

That's excellent advice.

11.

The Last Chapter
For Now...

*He must believe and not doubt, because he who doubts will be blown and tossed by
the wind.*
James 1:6

Since Hurricane Hugo, South Carolina's coast has been menaced (but
not seriously injured) by hurricanes like Bertha and Fran in 1996,
Bonnie in 1998, Floyd in 1999, Charley (with eighty mile per hour winds)
on August 14, 2004, and Gaston two weeks later (with wind clocked at
seventy-five miles per hour). Meanwhile, the amount of development along
the coast has continued to increase. South Carolina's subtropical climate
is very attractive to retirees seeking to escape from colder northern climes.

The value of insured residential property in the coastal counties of
South Carolina now is close to $100 billion dollars. That figure represents
only those homes, condominiums and time-shares that are insured in
counties that abut the Atlantic Ocean, not those a little further away. But as
meteorological history reveals, hurricanes can cause tremendous damage a
hundred miles or more inland.

So where does all this leave us?

One of America's first scientists specializing in long range forecasting is
Professor William Gray of Colorado State University. He is of the belief
that "[t]he whole East Coast was very lucky for the past 30 or 40 years."[155]
He believes that things are getting a lot worse. After a lull in activity, the pace
of storms in the Atlantic Ocean picked up in 1995. Since then, the number

of powerful storms has about doubled. While many of those storms stayed out at sea (and, by doing that, generated little anxiety and even less media attention) the fact that cyclonic activity is on the upswing is very disturbing on many levels.

One group of people who are very worried about this trend in the weather are those who bet (and make a lot of money) on storms. With approximately 5.5 trillion dollars in insured property (residential, commercial and industrial) at risk to hurricanes along the Atlantic seaboard and in the Gulf of Mexico, insurance companies have a great deal to either gain or lose based on their odds makers' prognostications.

In order to ensure that they are winners, not losers, in their gigantic gambling enterprise, insurers scour the work of meteorologists, climatologists and other scientists looking for information that will help in setting the odds or, in insurance language, "properly calculate premiums."

Part of their calculations takes into account the sixty- to seventy-year cycle of storm activity known as the Atlantic Multidecadal Oscillation. The engine of this up-and-down cycle is fueled by salinity and sea surface temperatures in which higher temperatures correlate to increased storm activity. These conditions play a significant role in running the Atlantic conveyor belt, a part of a much larger system of ocean currents. The world's oceans continuously circulate. Surface water is warmed by the tropical sun and flows north toward the poles. Once it reaches the arctic, the water cools down and sinks. That cooler water then flows back to the tropics in deepwater currents.

Higher air temperatures have the apparent effect of speeding up this circulation. The increase in circulation spawns more storm activity. According to recent measures of such things, this conveyor belt's cycle appears to be in an upswing. "The warmer the sea-surface temperature and the more warm, moist air that's available, the stronger a hurricane can become," meteorologist Chris Landsea of NOAA's Hurricane Research Division told National Geographic magazine last year.[156]

That information, by itself, might be enough to motivate the actuaries (odds makers) at insurance companies to demand more money from their customers. But insurers want to know even more. Because they do, the large companies are funding much of the research coming from the fledgling science of paleotempestology: a study of ancient hurricane activity by looking at the geological record.

As it turns out, evidence of ancient hurricanes can be found in the sediments and fossils found inside otherwise quiet coastal environments. Sand layers laid down by massive hurricanes in coastal lakes and marshes leave telltale strata. These are the result of hurricane storm surges flowing over shoreline sand dunes, carrying with them salt and sand from the ocean, along with organic matter. When the water retreats back to the sea, the deposits are left behind. Over time, these are covered by the natural processes otherwise taking place on shore. Distinctive layers result. By carbon dating these layers, a history of ancient, intense storm activity can be rewritten for the past five thousand years or longer.[157]

Funded largely by the insurance industry's "Risk Prediction Initiative," the fledgling science of paleotempestology has been seeking data from sites from Texas to Massachusetts, including sites at Folly Beach, Middleton Pond (birthplace of Pawleys Island's Gray Man) in Georgetown County and Myrtle Beach, South Carolina.

The technique is straightforward. Core samples are drilled at promising sites in coastal freshwater lakes and marshes. The layers are separated and the organic and chemical composition of each is studied. Those layers with the distinctive components left behind by storm surges are carbon dated. From this information a timetable listing the history of catastrophic storms can be obtained. The data collected so far has been promising.

"There are millennial-scale variations in hurricane activity," Dr. Lambiu Liu of Louisiana State University and a pioneer in this scientific effort has said.[158]

> *Our data suggest that there are much longer cycles superimposed on the decadal cycles. We've had a quiet period, an active period, and for the past 1,000 years, we're back to a relatively quiet period.*
>
> *Indeed, the data indicates that catastrophic hurricanes struck the Gulf Coast much more frequently 1,000 to 3,500 years ago than they do now. During that hyperactive period, such storms hit the area from four to five times more often than they have in the past 1,000 years.*

The forecast? Two things: First, there is the sure bet. Based on the available scientific data, insurance premiums, both for homeowners insurance covering wind damage and flood insurance covering water damage (neither type covers both losses), will increase, and do so dramatically in the next several years. They will because insurance companies are not in the business of losing money. They understand that the risk of loss is about to rise sharply.

So like any other bookie, they will set the odds (premiums) to ensure that they will not lose in the long run. They may stop betting on the risk. But if they bet, they will profit.

The second forecast is almost as certain. We are all in for quite a ride.

Epilogue

All things are woven in a silken web
Each strand entwined with the others
Gently pluck a single strand
Resonate the others.[159]

As the twentieth century came to a close, scientists and politicians argued about whether human activity was causing the earth to get warmer. To find out, the Artic Climate Impact Assessment has been conducted. It involved drilling core samples from glaciers, arctic ice and sea beds to obtain a climate history going back a half million years. Among other things, this study concluded that today's levels of carbon dioxide (a principal greenhouse gas) are higher than they have been in hundreds of thousands of years.

Based on the ever-growing body of evidence, prominent scientists have cautioned that accumulating greenhouse gases are causing a serious environmental problem. Whether unable to comprehend the science or unwilling to offend corporate contributors, politicians responded in their customary fashion. They point to so-called "gaps" in scientific knowledge and continue to deny that a problem exists. They continue doing so as the gaps in understanding become narrower and narrower and the evidence connecting human activity and global warming has mounted.

Earth scientists now project that all arctic ice will be gone before the end of this century, or earlier. In fact, according to President Reagan's former science advisor, even if all human-generated global warming activity were to stop immediately, the forecast is that the earth's climate will continue to warm the planet for hundreds of years to come.[160]

At a geophysics conference in New Orleans in May of 2005, Dr. James W. Hurrell, a scientist associated with the National Center for Atmospheric Research in Boulder, Colorado, presented findings of a long-term study of ocean warming on weather patterns. The study included a thorough review of twentieth century historical record of changes in ocean temperatures and weather patterns. Using that data, sixty separate computer simulations of climate change were run. To assure there would be no bias in outcomes, five separate computer models were used. Each model was conceived and programmed at a separate research center.

The historical data established that the temperature of the world's oceans has been rising steadily. These increases correlated with increases in industrial activity and rising in the burning of fossil fuels. They also established that warming seawater causes changes in air circulation. As ocean water gets warmer, the air above does too. The warm air rises, carrying water vapor with it. As the warm, wet air rises and it comes into contact with cooler air. The water vapor condenses and rain falls. That rain cools flowing air masses below, dropping the moisture back into the sea before it reaches land. The result: the air is drier as it passes over adjacent land, resulting in less rain for crops.[161]

The consequence of this dynamic process to humans can be dramatic. "When rains fail, people die" is the way Dr. Richard Washington of Oxford put it.[162] Speaking on a different, but interrelated, geologic subject, Dr. Michael E. West, a seismologist at the Alaska Volcano Observatory aptly observed, "We're learning the earth is a far more connected place than we once thought it was."[163]

No matter where the heads of politicians may be buried, there is no longer any serious dispute in the scientific community but that the environment is growing steadily warmer. Fully 98 percent of the world's glaciers are melting. Polar ice caps are melting. The year 2005 was marked by the largest retreat of arctic sea ice in history.[164] According to a joint study of satellite data compiled over a ten-year period starting in 1996, NASA's Jet Propulsion Laboratory in Pasadena, California, and the University of Kansas, found that the massive, seven hundred thousand square mile, two mile thick glaciers of Greenland are shrinking faster than ever before. If this melts, sea levels around the world could rise by as much as twenty feet.[165] This sort of melting has caused the northern ring of the Gulf Stream to shut down in the past, cutting off the flow of cooling arctic waters into the southern Atlantic, causing the Caribbean to heat up and freezing Europe at the same time.

The average temperatures of the seas are rising. Evidence gathered by paleoclimatologists reveals that the sharpest increases in two millennia began sometime around 1990.[166] While the earth has experienced warm and cold cycles throughout geologic history, the pace of the current warming trend is much accelerated, fueled by the massive burning of tropical forests and an even more pervasive consumption of fossil fuels. These changes in sea levels, sea temperatures, sea currents and weather patterns can prove to be very disruptive of human society, in many ways, including by fueling more frequent and violent tropical cyclones.

A very significant part of human economic activity is conducted in coastal cities. A large part of the world's population lives on vulnerable land located at or near sea level. A rise in sea level threatens those populations and the business they conduct. (Imagine what will be left of South Carolina's coastal cities and towns if the Atlantic Ocean rises twenty feet.) At the same time, the droughts brought on by the interaction of increased sea temperatures, air circulation, oceanic rainfall and drier prevailing winds over land could drastically affect food production around the globe.

To the earth itself, these changes are insignificant. It has gone through dramatic climate shifts many times during the three and a half billion years since it was first formed. The most recent great heat wave, the Paleocene Eocene Thermal Maximum, occurred some fifty-five million years ago. The earth survived it. Some species did too. Others did not. But since that temperature rise was a gradual one occurring over tens of thousands of years, its effect on living things was gradual too. Today's temperature increases, on the other hand, are occurring much more rapidly. So, too, may be the consequences to mankind.

"All this global warming has nothing to do with the planet," climatologist Dr. David Barber of the University of Manitoba says. "The planet will go through its normal cycles, and it'll do its own thing. It only has to do with us—as people. Our economic side of things and our political side of things are really what are being affected by climate change. The planet could care less."[167]

While, in strictly scientific terms Dr. Barber is probably correct, Dwamish Chief Seattle expressed a more spiritual view. In reply to a treaty offer on behalf of his tribe he wrote,

Every part of the earth is sacred to my people. Every shining pine needle, every sandy shore, every mist in the dark woods, every clearing, and every humming insect is holy in the memory and experience of my people. The sap that courses through the trees carries the memories of the red man. So when the Great Chief in Washington sends word that he wishes to buy our land, he asks much of us...

This we know: All things are connected. Whatever befalls the earth befalls the sons of the earth. Man did not weave the web of life; he is merely a strand in it. Whatever he does to the web, he does to himself.

...to harm the earth is to heap contempt on its Creator. The whites too shall pass; perhaps sooner than all other tribes. Continue to contaminate your bed, and you will one night suffocate in your own waste.

But in perishing you will shine brightly, fired by the strength of the God who brought you to this land and for some special purpose gave you dominion over this land and over the red man. That destiny is a mystery to us, for we do not [know what will come] *when the buffalo are all slaughtered, the wild horses all tamed, and the view of the ripe hills blotted by talking wires. Where is the thicket? Gone. Where is the eagle? Gone. And what is it to say goodbye to the swift pony and the hunt? The end of living and the beginning of survival...*

If we agree [to sell the land], *it will be to secure the reservation you have promised. There, perhaps, we may live out our brief days as we wish. When the last red man has vanished from the earth, and his memory is only the shadow of a cloud moving across the prairie, those shores and forest will still hold the spirits of my people. For we love this earth as a newborn loves its mother's heartbeat. So if we sell our land, love it as we've loved it. Care for it as we've cared for it. Hold in your mind the memory of the land as it is when you take it. And preserve it for your children, and love it...as God loves us all.*

...[O]*ur God is the same God. This earth is precious to Him. Even the white man cannot be exempt from the common destiny. We may be brothers after all. We shall see.*

Epilogue

Since this treaty was made, the buffalo were slaughtered. Wild horses were tamed. Trees were felled. Thickets were cleared. Wires were strung everywhere. Factories were built. Cars burned trillions of gallons of fossil fuel. The air filled with soot and smoke and smog.

Chief Seattle said that this would all produce the end of life and the beginning of a struggle for survival. Hosea put it another way. He prophesied that those who have "sown the wind, shall reap the whirlwind."[168]

Appendix

Number of hurricanes affecting South Carolina per decade, 1800 to 2000:

1800	4*	1910	2
1810	4*	1920	1
1820	3*	1930	1
1830	4	1940	2
1840	1	1950	6*
1850	2	1960	1
1860	1	1970	2
1870	2	1980	3*
1880	4	1990	3
1890	7*		
1900	3		

*One or more catergory three storms occurred in these decades: 1804, 1813, 1822, two storms in 1893, 1954, 1959 and 1989.

Notes

Chapter 1

[1] Andrew Philips and Sue Ferguson, *A Stormy Season: Why Big Hurricanes Like Floyd Are on the Rise*, MacLeans, September 27, 1999.

[2] NOAA, nhc.noaa.gov.

[3] Low-pressure doldrums that shift up and down across the equator and "midatlantic weather disturbances" drawn to the equator from subtropical seas can also result in a hurricane.

[4] "El Niño and Africa's Food," Science Times, *New York Times,* February 21, 2006.

[5] Ibid.

[6] NOAA, "The Deadliest Atlantic Tropical Cyclones, 1492–1996," nhc.noaa.gov/pastdeadly.shtml.

Chapter 2

[7] Raccolta di Documenti et Studi pubblicatia dalla R. Commissione Columbiana (Rome 1892–94) in Samuel E. Morrison, *Admiral of the Ocean Sea; A Life of Christopher Columbus, Volume II,* (Boston, 1942), 241–242.

[8] David M. Ludlum, *Early American Hurricanes* (Boston, 1963), 3.

[9] Morrison, *Admiral of the Ocean Sea*, 243.

[10] Ludlum, *Early American Hurricanes*, 3.

[11] Ibid.

[12] Ibid.

[13] Ferdinand Columbus, *The Life of the Admiral Columbus*. Ed. and trans. by

Benjamin Keen (New Brunswick: 1959; First published 1571), 179.

[14] Ludlum, *Early American Hurricanes*, 6.

[15] Ibid.

[16] Kerry Emanuel, *Divine Wind, The History and Science of Hurricanes* (New York, 2005), 30.

[17] Cecil Jane, *The Voyages of Christopher Columbus,* London, 1930, at 293.

[18] Columbus, *Life of Admiral Columbus*, 229.

[19] Ibid., 246.

[20] Ibid.

[21] G. Benzoni, *History of the New World, 1541 to 1556,* (New York, 1970); Emanuel, *Divine Wind*, 32.

Chapter 3

[22] Woodbury Lowery, *The Spanish Settlements in the United States, 1531–1561* in Ludlum, *Early American Hurricanes*, 8.

[23] Lawrence Rowland, Alexander Moore and George C. Rogers Jr., *The History of Beaufort County, South Carolina* (Columbia, 1996), 26–28.

[24] David Beers, *The Roanoke Voyages, 1584–1590, Series 2, Volume 104* in Ludlum, *Early American Hurricanes*, 9.

[25] Ibid.

[26] Ibid.

[27] Ibid.

[28] Thomas Southey, *Chronological History of the West Indies* (London, 1827) in Ludlum, *Early American Hurricanes*.

Chapter 4

[29] Walter Edgar, *South Carolina, A History* (Columbia, 1998), 2.

[30] William Bartram, *Diary of a Journey through the Carolinas, Georgia and Florida from July 1, 1765, to April 10, 1766.* Edited by Francis Harper (The American Philosophical Society, 1942), 20.

[31] T.J. Westenbaker, *Virginia under the Stuarts, 1607–1688,* quoting a letter from Secretary Thomas Ludwell to Lord Berkeley in Ludlum, *Early American Hurricanes*, 15.

[32] Rowland, Moore and Rogers, *History of Beaufort County*, 72–75.

[33] Ibid., 73.

[34] Ibid., 74.

[35] Ibid., 73.

[36] Paper to the Lords Proprietor c. 1686, quoted by J.G. Dunlop, *South Carolina Historical & Genealogical Magazine*, 1929, 83–84 in Ludlum, *Early American Hurricanes*, 42.

[37] Some accounts date the "rice storm" a year earlier in 1685. This writer found no reliable record of a storm near South Carolina that year, but only a record for the following year, 1686.

[38] James Percival Petit, *South Carolina and the Sea*, Volume I (Charleston, 1986), 39.

[39] Ibid.

[40] Ibid.

[41] David Ramsey, *History of South Carolina*, Volume II (Newbury, SC, 1858), 176.

[42] George C. Rogers Jr., *The History of Georgetown County, South Carolina* (Columbia, 1970), 10.

[43] Ibid.; Also Hugh T. Lefler, ed., *A New Voyage to Carolina by John Lawson* (Chapel Hill, 1967), 18–19; Anne King Gregorie, *Notes on Seewee Indians and Indian Remains of Christ Church Parish* (Charleston, 1925), 10–11.

Chapter 5

[44] Ibid.

[45] The date is from the Julian calendar. On the Gregorian calendar, it would be September 16 and 17, 1713.

[46] Mark Catesby, *Natural History of Carolina, Florida and the Bahama Islands* (London, 1731), ii in Ludlum, *Early American Hurricanes*, 43.

[47] Ramsey, *History of South Carolina*, 175–176n; Ludlum, *Early American Hurricanes*, 43.

[48] Letter from Le Jau to the Secretary of St. James Parish dated January 22, 1713, as reprinted in *The Carolina Chronicle of Dr. Francis Le Jau*, F.J. Klingberg, ed. (University of California Press, 1956), 136.

[49] Ludlum, *Early American Hurricanes*, 60.

[50] Ibid., 61.

[51] G.R. Frick and R.P. Stearns, *Mark Catesby, Colonial Audubon* (Urbana, IL, 1961), 24 in Ludlum *Early American Hurricanes*, 61.

[52] Ibid.

[53] Ibid., 44.

[54] Walter Isaacson, *Benjamin Franklin* (New York, 2003).

[55] See, in addition to the *South Carolina Gazette*, Elmer D. Johnson & Kathleen Lewis Sloan, *South Carolina, A Documentary Profile of the Palmetto State* (Columbia,

1971); Petit, *South Carolina and the Sea*, 66.

[56] Edgar, *South Carolina*, 161.

[57] Ludlum, *Early American Hurricanes*, 44.

[58] *South Carolina Gazette* (Charleston), September 14, 1769.

[59] Ludlum, *Early American Hurricanes*, 26–27.

[60] Ibid., 50.

[61] *U.S. Chronicle* (Providence), November 28, 1792.

[62] *N.Y. Gazette*, November 22, 1797, in Ludlum, *Early American Hurricanes*, 52.

Chapter 6

[63] Ibid.

[64] Matthew L. Davis, ed., *Memoirs of Aaron Burr*, quoted in Ludlum, *Early American Hurricanes*, 53.

[65] Ibid.

[66] Ibid., 54.

[67] Ibid., 56.

[68] *Wilmington Gazette*, (Wilmington, NC), August 26, 1806.

[69] Ludlum, *Early American Hurricanes*, 56.

[70] *Charleston Times*, September 11, 1811.

[71] Rogers, *History of Georgetown County*, 196–197.

[72] Petit, *South Carolina and the Sea*, 36.

[73] Rogers, *History of Georgetown County*, 197.

[74] Rowland, Moore and Rogers, *History of Beaufort County*, 289.

[75] "Dear John, Charleston, August 29, 1823," *U.S. Gazette*, September 19, 1813.

[76] *Charleston City Gazette*, August 31, 1813.

[77] Rogers, *History of Georgetown County*, 224–225.

[78] *U.S. Gazette*, September 14, 1813.

[79] Ludlum, *Early American Hurricanes*, 112.

Chapter 7

[80] Ibid., 114.

[81] The scientific theory of the day was that hurricanes were caused by the sun's crossing of the equator at the autumn equinox.

[82] *Charleston Courier*, September 30, 1822.

[83] *Charleston Gazette*, October 3, 1822.

[84] Ibid.

[85] Ludlum, *Early American Hurricanes*, 115.

[86] Samuel D. McGill, *Narrative Reminiscences in Williamsburg County* (Kingstree, SC, 1952), 10.

[87] Ibid., 9.

[88] Ibid., 10.

[89] Ibid., 9

[90] E.M. Betts, *Thomas Jefferson's Garden Book, 1766–1824,* maintained as part of the Nicolas Trist Papers in the Library of Congress, in Ludlum, *Early American Hurricanes*, 116.

[91] Ibid.

[92] *Monthly Weather Review* (Washington, D.C.), May 1896.

[93] Nancy Roberts, *Ghosts of the Carolinas* (Columbia, 1962); Nancy Roberts, *Ghosts from the Coast* (Chapel Hill, 2001).

[94] *State Gazette* (Columbia), September 17, 1824.

[95] Edgar, *South Carolina*, 273.

[96] Washington, D.C.'s *National Journal* of June 14, 1825, in Ludlum, *Early American Hurricanes*, 87 and 119.

[97] Ibid.; *Charleston Mercury*, June 14, 1825.

[98] Ibid.

[99] Ibid.

[100] Ludlum, *Early American Hurricanes*, 88; *National Journal* (New York), June 7, 1825; *Charleston Mercury*, June 14, 1825.

[101] Ludlum, *Early American Hurricanes*, 119.

[102] Tom Rubillo, *Trial and Error* (Charleston: The History Press, 2005), 29–31, citing *Kinloch v. Harvey,* Harp. 509 (1830).

[103] Ludlum, *Early American Hurricanes*, 121.

[104] *Winyah Intelligencer* (Georgetown), August 19, 1830, and August 21, 1930; Ludlum, *Early American Hurricanes*, 121.

[105] Ludlum, *Early American Hurricanes*, 121.

[106] *Charleston Courier*, September 5, 1834.

[107] *Charleston Courier*, September 5, 1834.

[108] Ludlum, *Early American Hurricanes*, 145–146.

[109] Ibid.

Chapter 8

[110] Ludlum, *Early American Hurricanes*, 158, 160.

[111] Ibid., 133.

[112] J.H. Easterby, ed., *The South Carolina Rice Plantation* (Chicago, 1945), 408.

[113] Ludlum, *Early American Hurricanes*, 172.

[114] Ibid., 134–135; Gary Kinder, *Ship of Gold in the Deep Blue Sea* (Thorndike, ME, 1998), 128.

[115] NOAA, "The Deadliest Atlantic Tropical Cyclones, 1492–1996," nhc.noaa.gov/pastdeadly.shtml.

[116] Ludlum, *Early American Hurricanes*, 101.

[117] Petit, *South Carolina and the Sea*, 91.

[118] Ibid.

[119] Ibid., 92.

Chapter 9

[120] Ibid., 148–149.

[121] Christopher C. Boyle and James A. Fitch, ed., *Georgetown County Slave Narratives* (Georgetown, SC, 1998), 37.

[122] Ibid., 35.

[123] Ibid., 36.

[124] *Charleston Yearbook, 1885.*

[125] Petit, *South Carolina and the Sea*, 158.

[126] Edgar, *South Carolina*, 426.

[127] "Saved from the Savannah," *The State* (Columbia), September 2, 1893.

[128] "The Greatest Storm; What Happened in Charleston, Savannah, Sullivan's Island, etc., etc.," *Georgetown Times*, September 2, 1893.

[129] *Georgetown Times*, August 30, 1893.

[130] Ibid., September 16, 1893.

[131] Ibid.

[132] Ibid.

[133] Boyle and Fitch, *Georgetown County Slave Narratives*, 43.

[134] Annie W. Weston Smoak, *News and Courier* (Charleston), October 13, 1933.

[135] Charles Winston Joyner, *The State* magazine (Columbia), January 16, 1983.

[136] Ibid.

[137] Ibid.

[138] Smoak, *News and Courier*.

[139] Letter from F.L. Guerry of Waverly Mills to Edmund N. Joyner dated October 16, 1893, reprinted in the *Georgetown Times*, October 21, 1893.

[140] Letter courtesy of the *Georgetown Times*.

[141] Undated and unsigned letter courtesy of the *Georgetown Times*.

[142] Letter of Dr. J. William Folk, October 13, 1893, reprinted in the *Georgetown Times*, October 21, 1893.

[143] Ibid.

[144] Boyle and Fitch, *Georgetown County Slave Narratives*, 36.

Chapter 10

[145] *Georgetown Times*, June 24, 2005.

[146] *Charleston News and Courier*, July 22, 1911.

[147] One other early twentieth century storm is worth noting. It occurred on October 19, 1910. While it caused no serious damage ashore, it took sixty-four lives at sea, including from ships that called Port Royal home. The storm had originated in the Gulf of Mexico below Cuba. It followed a track that carried it through the Yucatan channel. There, two steamers, the *Crown Prince* and the *Bluefields*, were struck. The *Crown Prince* had sailed from Santos with a cargo of 75,000 bags of coffee and was overdue in Port Royal when the news of her loss arrived. She had a crew of thirty-five. The *Bluefields* had a gross ton register of 1,002 tons and was loaded with bananas from Honduras. She had a crew of twenty-nine. In addition, the captain's wife was on board. All these souls were lost.

[148] *The State*, October 16, 1954.

[149] Hurricane Hazel, www.disastershq.com/features/hazel.asp.

[150] *Beaufort Gazette*, October 3, 1959.

[151] "Hurricane Hugo, A Diary of Destruction," *Charleston News and Courier*, September 29, 1989.

[152] "Medical Examiner/Coroner Reports of Deaths Associated with Hurricane Hugo—South Carolina," *Journal of the American Medical Association* (December 8, 1989).

[153] "Hugo Was a Wimp at Charleston, Scientists Warn," *Charleston Post and Courier*, July 25, 2000.

[154] Recollection of South Carolina Family Court Judge H.E. Bonnoitt Jr. as related to Hal M. Strange, Esquire of the Georgetown County Bar Association. Hal Strange later told the story to this author.

Chapter 11

[155] "In Hot Water," *National Geographic*, August 2005, 76.

[156] Ibid., 79.

[157] Kerry Emanuel, *Anthropogenic Effects on Tropical Cyclone Activity* (Cambridge: Massachusetts Institute of Technology) Center for Meteorology and Physical Oceanography; John Travis, "Hunting Prehistoric Hurricanes," *Science News*, May 20, 2000; Scott P. Hippensteel, Ronald E. Martin and M. Scott Harris; "Records of prehistoric hurricanes on the South Carolina coast based on micropalentological and sediment logical evidence, with comparison to other Atlantic Coast records; Discussion," Geological Society of America.

[158] Travis, "Hunting Prehistoric Hurricanes," 4.

Epilogue

[159] Poem of the author entitled *Seattle*.

[160] "60 Minutes," (Columbia Broadcasting System), February 19, 2006.

[161] Andrew C. Revkin, "Ocean Warmth Tied to African Drought," *New York Times*, May 24, 2005.

[162] Ibid.

[163] Kenneth Chang, "Post-Tsunami Earthquakes Rumbled Around the Globe," *New York Times*, May 24, 2005.

[164] Andrew C. Revkin, "Past Hot Times Hold Few Reasons to Relax About New Warming," *New York Times*, December 27, 2005.

[165] "Glaciers Flow to Sea at a Faster Pace, Study Says," *New York Times*, February 17, 2006.

[166] Ibid.

[167] Ibid.

[168] Hosea 8:7.

Bibliography

Anthes, R.A. *Tropical cyclones, their evolution, structure and effects*. Boston: American Meteorological Society, 1982.

Bartram, William. *Diary of a Journey through the Carolinas, Georgia and Florida from July 1, 1765, to April 10, 1766*. Edited by Francis Harper. Washington, D.C.: American Philosophical Society, 1942.

Benzoni, G. *History of the New World*. New York: Franklin, 1970.

Boyle, Christopher C., and James A. Fitch, ed. *Georgetown County Slave Narratives*. Georgetown: Georgetown County Rice Museum, 1998.

Columbus, Ferdinand. *The Life of Admiral Columbus*. 1571. Trans. and ed. by Benjamin Keen. New Brunswick: Rutgers University Press, 1959.

Conrad, James. *Typhoon and other stories*. New York: Sun Dial Press, 1938.

Easterby, J.H., ed. *The South Carolina Rice Plantation*. Chicago: University of Illinois Press, 1945.

Edgar, Walter. *South Carolina, A History*. Columbia: University of South Carolina Press, 1998.

Emanuel, Kerry. *Divine Wind, The History and Science of Hurricanes*. New York: Oxford University Press, 2005.

———. "Anthropogenic Effects on Tropical Cyclone Activity." http://wind.mit.edu/-emanuel/anthro.

Gregorie, Anne King. *Notes on Seewee Indians and Indian Remains of Christ Church Parish*. Charleston, 1925.

Isaacson, Walter. *Benjamin Franklin*. New York: Simon & Schuster, 2003.

Jane, Cecil. *The Voyages of Christopher Columbus*. London, 1930.

Johnson, Elmer D., and Kathleen Lewis Sloan. *South Carolina, A Documentary Profile of the Palmetto State*. Columbia, 1971.

Kinder, Gary. *Ship of Gold in the Deep Blue Sea*. Thorndike, ME, 1998.

Klingberg, F.J., ed. *The South Carolina Chronicle of Dr. Francis Le Jau*. 1956.

Larson, E. Isaac's Storm: *A Man, a Time, and the Deadliest Hurricane in History*. New York: Crown Publishers, 1999.

Lefler, Hugh T., ed. *A New Voyage to Carolina by John Lawson*. Chapel Hill,: University of North Carolina Press, 1967.

Ludlum, David M. *Early American Hurricanes*. Boston: American Meteorological Society, 1963.

Maslin, Mark. *Global Warming; A Very Short Introduction*. Oxford: Oxford University Press, 2004.

McGill, Samuel D. *Narrative Reminiscences in Williamsburg County*. Columbia: The State Company, 1923.

Morrison, Samuel E. *Admiral of the Ocean Sea, A Life of Christopher Columbus*. Boston, 1942.

Petit, James Percival. *South Carolina and the Sea*, Volume I. Charleston, 1986.

Philips, Andrew, and Sue Ferguson. *A Stormy Season: Why Big Hurricanes Like Floyd Are on the Rise*.

Bibliography

Ramsey, David. *History of South Carolina*. Newbury, 1858.

Roberts, Nancy. *Ghosts of the Carolinas*. Columbia: University of South Carolina Press, 1962.

―――. *Ghosts from the Coast*. Chapel Hill: University of North Carolina Press, 2001.

Rogers, George C. Jr. *The History of Georgetown County, South Carolina*. Columbia: University of South Carolina Press, 1970.

Rowland, Lawrence, Alexander Moore and George C. Rogers Jr. *The History of Beaufort County, South Carolina*. Columbia: University of South Carolina Press, 1996.

Rubillo, Tom. *Trial and Error.* Charleston: The History Press, 2005.

Southey, Thomas. *Chronological History of the West Indies*. London, 1827.

Newspapers

Camden Journal
Charleston Courier
Charleston City Gazette
Charleston Mercury
Charleston Post and Courier
Charleston Times
Georgetown Times
New York Times
News and Courier
State Gazette
The State
U.S. Chronicle
U.S. Gazette
Wilmington Gazette
Winyah Intelligencer

About the Author

Tom Rubillo is a retired attorney who lives in Georgetown, South Carolina. He is a survivor of hurricanes Hazel in 1954 and Hugo in 1989. This is his third book about local history. *Trial and Error* was published by The History Press in 2005. He is working on a Civil War history about Brigadier General Edward Potter's march from the coast of South Carolina in the last months of the war.

Visit us at
www.historypress.com